One Bread, One Body

D1473007

One Bread, One Body

The Ecumenical Experience of L'Arche

Thérèse Vanier

Novalis/Gracewing

One Bread, One Body:
The Ecumenical Experience of L'Arche
is published by Gracewing and Novalis Publishing.

© 1997

Front cover photo: L'Arche Trosly-Breuil
Photo of Dr. Vanier: Jonathan Lloyd
Interior photos: L'Arche Bouaké, Daybreak,
Lambeth, Trosly-Breuil, and Asha Niketan, Calcutta

Layout: Gilles Lépine

Scripture quotations are taken from
the Revised Standard Version of the Bible,
© 1966, unless otherwise stated.

Gracewing, Fowler Wright Books, 2 Southern Avenue,
Leominster, HR6 0QF
England

British Library Cataloguing-in-Publication Data
A record for this book is available from the British Library.
ISBN: 0-85244-422-2

Novalis Editorial Office
223 Main St., Ottawa, Ontario K1S 1C4

Novalis Business Office
49 Front St. East, 2nd Floor,
Toronto, Ontario M5E 1B3

Canadian Cataloguing-in-Publication Data
Vanier, Thérèse, 1923–
        One bread, one body: the ecumenical experience of L'Arche
Includes bibliographical references.
ISBN 2-89088-834-7
        1. Arche (Association) 2. Interdenominational
cooperation. 3. Catholic Church–Relations.
4. Religions–Relations. I. Title.
BX2347.8.M4V38   1997   267'.182   C97-900021-1

Printed in Canada

To all men and women who live, work
and pray for reconciliation:
all who seek to heal and to be healed

May oppressed people, and those who oppress them,
free each other
May those who are handicapped, and those who think
they are not,
help each other
May those who need someone to listen
touch the hearts of those who are too busy
May the homeless bring joy to those who open their doors
reluctantly
May the lonely heal those who think they are self-sufficient
May the poor melt the hearts of the rich
May seekers for truth give life
to those who are satisfied that they have found it
May the dying who do not wish to die be comforted
by those who find it hard to live
May the unloved be allowed
to unlock the hearts of those who cannot love
May prisoners find true freedom and liberate others from fear
May those who sleep on the streets share their gentleness
with those who cannot understand them
May the hungry tear the veil from the eyes of those
who do not hunger after justice
May those who live without hope cleanse the hearts
of their brothers and sisters who are afraid to live
May the weak confound the strong and save them
May violence be overcome by compassion
May violence be absorbed by men and women of peace
May violence succumb to those who are totally vulnerable

That we may be healed

Contents

Foreword

The word *ecumenism* comes from two Greek words meaning "house" and "dwell," and has come to mean "the whole inhabited earth." In the early days of the Christian church, the term "ecumenical council" referred to a gathering of all the bishops from "the inhabited earth."

Today the word is often given different interpretations: in Europe, it is in general taken to mean dialogue and movement towards unity between Christian churches. In North America, however, and certainly in some other parts of the world, it is generally understood to include dialogue with other faiths. The communities of l'Arche embrace people of different Christian traditions, those who belong to other World Faiths, and still others whose spirituality has no explicit foundation in any of the major religions. Within the context of l'Arche, therefore, the word ecumenism has the wider connotation of dialogue with other faiths.

For each l'Arche community ecumenism has been a matter of experience. "We became ecumenical when we welcomed men and women with a handicap who belonged to different denominations and different religions."[1]

As a member of l'Arche in the United Kingdom since 1972, I have limited personal experience of the wider dimension of our communities. This account is based very substantially upon our Christian interdenominational experience in the U.K. and is an

---

[1]   *Ecumenism in l'Arche* (1).

attempt to share my own experience and draw upon that of others in order to explore the ecumenical reality for our communities.

For over twenty years, when attending the Anglican eucharist I have found myself saying the words: "Though we are many, we are one body, because we all share in one bread,"[2] just before the moment of communion. I then ask for and receive a blessing, but not communion, because the rules of the Roman Catholic Church to which I belong do not permit this. This experience of the paradox and contradiction of division at the eucharist is extremely painful – painful for those who refuse the proffered bread and cup, painful for those who offer and are refused, and painful for those to whom the elements are not offered.... The human implications of offering or refusing nourishment dominate the minds and hearts of people who are experiencing it in a way that may not apply to those who face the situation intellectually, but without personal experience. This has been a formative experience for me, as it has for others in l'Arche. Without it, we would not have found ourselves part of a movement towards unity among Christians, nor would we have come to understand the nature of the bread we do share, an aspect which is developed in the last chapter of this book.

The family of l'Arche includes inter-faith communities in India and Africa. Therefore I have been able to include stories from different countries, stories which demonstrate how those who "live at the level of their hearts" bring us together, and how the otherwise "limited" symbol of bread, which is not the staple food everywhere in the world, nonetheless can include us all in our common humanity.

I would like to thank all who, over the years and for the purposes of this book, have shared their own stories and those of their communities, as well as their insights and experience: Dawn Barraqué, Hazel Bradley, Koffi Bragon, Helen Carron, Vincent Dunkling, Gabrielle Einsle, Barbara Fraughan, Eileen Glass, Christine and Tony Graff, Paul Harwood, Elizabeth Hunter, Dorothy Jayaraj, Antoine Kouagoué, Kunhikanaran, Doris Maxwell, Robert McWilliam, Sue Mosteller, Bertrand

---

2   Rite A, *The Alternative Service Book*, Church of England, 1980.

Peycelon, Beth Porter, Patrick Purnell, Tom Ryan, Chris Sadler, Maggie Smith, David Standley, Stephen Verney, and Philip Yates.

I am grateful to members of the l'Arche communities of Bouaké, Daybreak, Lambeth, Trosly-Breuil and Asha Niketan in Calcutta, who provided the photographs. Despite every effort, I was unable to trace the source of that on page 70: a sculpture in stone by Miss Julian Allan entitled "His left hand is under my head" (Song of Songs 2:6), which is at Sancta Maria Abbey, Nunraw, Haddington, Scotland.

The majority of photographs are included in the chapter on "Following the Signs" because this chapter refers to daily life in our communities, which these photographs illustrate.

Special gratitude goes to Donald Allchin and to Tom Ryan who, for very many years, have shared so much of their wisdom and spirit of reconciliation with l'Arche on its ecumenical journey.

I would also like to thank Donald Allchin and Gerald O'Collins, S.J., for their advice on the first draft of this book. Finally, my heartfelt thanks goes to Teresa de Bertodano who, throughout the writing of this book, encouraged and advised me with immense patience and skill.

For the sake of clarity I should mention that a community of l'Arche may vary in size from a single household – virtually always the case at the beginning – to some six or more households and a number of work areas.

Many different terms are used in the English-speaking world to refer to those who live at the level of their hearts because of their intellectual disability. Language is constantly shifting and this reflects attempts to respect and acknowledge the value of people with disabilities which put them at a severe disadvantage in our societies. I have used the term "people with mental handicap(s)" throughout the book.

Much of this material has appeared over the years in articles, documents, books and talks. Where there are omissions and inaccuracies, I ask those who may be hurt by them to recognize my goodwill as well as my limitations, and forgive me.

March 1996   *Thérèse Vanier*

1

The beginnings and signs on the way

L'Arche began in France in the 1960s in a particular Christian Roman Catholic soil and culture. The founders, Père Thomas Philippe and Jean Vanier, were deeply influenced by and rooted and nourished in the Roman Catholic faith. In 1964 and 1965 anyone visiting the original group in Trosly-Breuil would have had no doubt they were in a Roman Catholic community, albeit of an unusual kind.

However, enmeshed within the community was a strong, gospel-based, practical streak which of necessity went beyond denominational or religious boundaries. It was clear that the vision coming into being was rooted in the immediate and pressing needs of people with mental handicaps, rather than in the preliminary development of any spirituality or philosophy, or indeed any organization or structure.

Very soon, those belonging to Christian traditions other than Roman Catholic began to come to l'Arche and were welcomed as assistants. The people with handicaps were always welcomed regardless of religious affiliation. Inevitably the latter were representative of the majority of people in France and therefore belonged, at least nominally, to the Roman Catholic Church.

In 1969 the l'Arche community of Daybreak near Toronto was founded by Steve and Ann Newroth, both members of the Anglican Church of Canada; they were joined by members of the United Church of Canada and other churches of the Reformed tradition, as well as Roman Catholics. In 1970 the first community of Asha Niketan (Home of Hope) was founded in Bangalore, India, by Gabrielle Einsle, a Roman Catholic, and the majority of people with mental handicaps in the Indian community were of course Hindu. Thus the first interdenominational Christian community and the first inter-faith community were born before l'Arche had written its Charter to express the vision by which it sought to build and develop.

In 1974 a community opened in French-speaking West Africa, at Bouaké on Ivory Coast. Here people with handicaps who belonged to the Faith of Islam and others whose background was Animist – an awareness and cult of the spirit in all creation – became part of l'Arche. In the same year the first community opened in England, near Canterbury, the cradle of the Anglican communion.

Thus, without our consciously seeking it, l'Arche communities were bringing together people of different intellectual capacities belonging to different races, cultures, and classes, and also of differing Christian traditions and different World Faiths.

The late sixties and early seventies saw marked changes in the world which are still in process at the end of the twentieth century and which affected the development of l'Arche. The revolt of university students in 1968 was particularly dramatic in Paris but reverberated across the lives and attitudes of young people throughout the West. It was an upheaval which attracted people to our communities because part of the reverberation was an almost frantic search for community – for togetherness. Small Christian and secular communities sprang up like wildfire, many of them proving unable to sustain the initial impetus and therefore breaking up. Such attempts may well have been influenced by the isolating individualism which was creeping into society alongside the breakdown of family and marriage and an increasing insecurity at work.

At the same time the governments of several western countries were embarking upon new initiatives to improve the care of people with mental handicaps: "normalization" (the right of a person with a mental handicap to "a normal life") was taking root in North America and Scandinavia, while in the U.K. the government published a document in 1971 entitled "Better Services for the Mentally Handicapped" and welcomed the collaboration of organizations such as l'Arche.

In the Christian world the documents of the Second Vatican Council, and in particular the *Decree on Ecumenism*, were changing the face of the Roman Catholic Church. In 1971 a key paper was issued by the World Council of Churches, entitled *The Unity of the Church and the Handicapped in Society*. Although this and subsequent publications dealt largely with physical disability, there was a clear message regarding the place of all people with disabilities as an authentic Christian witness. In a chapter entitled "Not Whole without the Handicapped," Lesslie Newbigin writes:

> Those who are handicapped, oppressed, deprived are utterly indispensable to the Church's authentic life, not simply as those on behalf of whom the Church is called to labour in healing and in action for justice, but as those who *now*, as deprived and handicapped within the membership of the Church, have a part to play, and a witness to give, without which the Church will simply not be fully Christian.... For it is only when the witness of those who are handicapped is an integral part of the witness of the whole Church, that this witness is true to the Gospel of the Crucified who is risen, the risen Lord who is the Crucified. Only with this witness as part of its total message does the Church's message measure up to the heights and depths of the human situation.[3]

Communities of l'Arche came into being because the founders of each one had been touched by the vision of a new form of community, with people with mental handicaps at its heart – the needy and powerless. The vision was firmly rooted in the Christian Gospels and in each case the hearts of the founders had been touched by a retreat given by Jean Vanier, or by the first Faith and Light international pilgrimage to Lourdes in 1971,[4] with its revelation of the suffering of thousands of people with mental handicaps and their families.

---

3 *Partners in Life.*
4 Faith and Light, also founded by Jean Vanier, brings together non-residential communities of children and adults with mental handicaps, their families and friends.

There is ambiguity in the term "needy and powerless," because the perceived needs of such people are in fact the deepest needs of every human being: to be loved and to love, to belong and to be valued for who one is. And it is the particular powerlessness of people with mental handicaps which has the power either to touch and liberate hearts, or else disturb and destroy and thus oblige others to defend themselves, building barriers around their own hearts. In those early days I doubt if anyone would have articulated things in this way, but the reality was already being sensed and experienced at an increasingly conscious level.

The first Charter of l'Arche was written for the Asha Niketan communities in India in 1970 in order to enshrine the vision of l'Arche in an Indian and inter-faith context. This was necessary as part of the legal documentation required in India by the State in order that the communities might exist officially. The Charter for Christian communities in the western world only came to be written in 1971, but both Charters made it clear that people are welcomed to the communities regardless of religious affiliation.

Looking back on the early days of these first communities, we can piece together a number of incidents and circumstances which indicated our ecumenical way forward.

Gabrielle, who founded the first Indian community, describes their beginnings:

"Go and tell what you hear and see" was Jesus' answer to John the Baptist, who had sent his disciples from his prison to ask: "Are you he who is to come or shall we look for another?" To people, be they Hindus, Christians, Moslems or persons with no particular ties to a religion, asking us what we stood for when we started l'Arche in Bangalore in 1970 we could only point to what we saw happening:

It was Gurunathan and Joe-boy, then Srinivas, Somasundra, Narasingha, Mohanraj, Lenny, George, Shyam who allowed us to experience something quite unheard of in India, where different categories of people are used to sticking to their place, fixed by tradition and customs. I am still amazed when I remember the liberty we took to invite anyone without much ado to eat with us on the floor of Asha

Niketan; men, women, our gardener, who must have been a Harijan,[5] professionals from our Governing Body, priests, Brahmins,[6] Muslims…. Is it because it made absolutely no sense to Srinivas, whose heart is much too big for his brain, to distinguish people in terms of a particular profession, cast or religion? He certainly was a barometer to register anyone's tendency to exclude or hurt others! Gandhi, in whom we discovered a real brother, certainly was a reference to help people understand what we were doing.

It must be said that our confidence in starting a home with mentally handicapped people, whose language and traditions we did not know, was based on the beatitudes. We counted on the promise of Jesus "Blessed are the poor." And, notwithstanding their background or religion, blessed indeed they were in leading us in ways which we could not imagine in advance.

We lived a telling demonstration of that in our prayer room, where Jean Vanier, Ronald from Canada and I had started to gather morning and evening in front of a little cross and an icon of Mary, a few days prior to the arrival of Guru-nathan and Joe-boy. Guru happened to come from a traditional Hindu family, whereas Joe was a Catholic. He promptly added St. Antony next to Mary and completed our song repertory with "Soul of my Saviour." From his first weekend back with his family, Guru came with the picture of his favourite god, proudly introducing us to Murugha. There followed other deities, as the family expanded through new admissions: Lord Shiva came along through Srinivas, Lord Ganesha through Mohanraj, who also introduced us to his favourite bahjans (religious songs), and Lenny contributed a glittering rosary.

I shall never forget the surprise of a visiting Indian Cardinal. Shyam had taken him straight away to our prayer room, keen to show our "pictures," all duly garlanded with fresh flowers. My story of how the collection "happened" may have helped the Cardinal, as guardian of my own faith,

---

5   These people were known pejoratively as "outcast."
6   This is the highest Hindu cast.

to appreciate Shyam's eagerness to acquaint him with our need to worship God. But it left him with the same questions as we ourselves were to face and which called us to greater clarity in an interreligious dialogue.

Back in the West, Sue Mosteller, a Canadian Roman Catholic sister who joined the Daybreak community near Toronto in 1972, describes contacts in those early days with local Anglican, Roman Catholic and United churches, and the Confirmation of Anglican members of the community with mental handicaps. She also describes the questions and the pain surrounding celebration of the eucharist in the community. In her community, they had presumed that it was acceptable to offer eucharistic hospitality to whomever chose to come forward at the time of communion and therefore no clear decisions were made regarding who could, or could not, receive communion. A number of Anglican and Roman Catholic ministers visited the community, sometimes for long periods, and were happy to celebrate and to share the eucharist with believing Christians who wished to receive, and on the whole people received if they wished and if that felt right to them.

This would certainly have been the pattern in the early days for several communities in Canada and the United States. Some years later, at retreats organized by l'Arche or other groups with which l'Arche was connected, participants were asked to respect the rules of the Roman Catholic Church.[7] People with mental handicaps could not understand and felt left out, while assistants were hurt and frequently angry.

Roman Catholics who came to the Daybreak community, and whose only experience of l'Arche was in Trosly with its strong tradition of daily eucharist and reservation of the blessed sacrament wanted the same thing in Canada, which led to friction in the interdenominational and Canadian culture which saw this as too Catholic and very foreign.

In 1974 Dawn Barraqué founded the first community of l'Arche in Africa, in Bouaké on the Ivory Coast. She writes:

---

7   See p. 61.

6

The founding members included two men with mental handicaps: Seydou, who was a Muslim originally from Nigeria and N'Goran who was from an Animist background. Assistants came from both Catholic and Protestant backgrounds. The President of the Board of Directors was a practising Catholic and the Vice president a well-known Muslim doctor. These differences, encountered very early on, helped us to discover the marked diversity of the local population, with its many ethnic and religious groups.

Welcoming each person into the community meant helping each one to find his or her way within it, in daily life and in the local events of Bouaké. Seydou had his prayer mat in his own room so that he could say his prayer whenever he wanted and we took him each Friday to the mosque for the weekly prayer gathering. The Muslim feast days were national holidays and we all accompanied Seydou when he joined the countless people, beautifully dressed, coming from all directions to the mosque. It was a breathtaking sight: people of all ages, as far as the eye could see, a blanket of silence, all standing, kneeling, praying together.

When Seydou died in 1980 he was buried by his Muslim friends who came and themselves saw to everything, so that the funeral rites were carried out according to his Muslim faith.

The time of prayer in the community was important for Amouin and Bakari, who were children in those early years. At one period the team of assistants had difficulty being faithful to this time every evening, feeling that it was demanding and lacked spontaneity. But every night after the evening meal, Amouin would go directly to the chapel and start to light the candle. Someone would follow her quickly to prevent her using up all the matches – or actually burning down the chapel; since she had only one good arm and partial use of the other, lighting the candle was not easy! Amouin would sit and wait peacefully with such a lovely smile – until everyone came. And then Bakari would clap his hands to begin the lively African version of the prayer of l'Arche. Amouin would clap also and Gilbert would begin the "Our Father." Little by little the team of assistants realized the importance of prayer at the heart of community life. Above all we discovered the importance of Amouin with her enthusiastic and yet peaceful mode of "preparing the way" and then waiting for us.

In the same year –1974 – those in the new community in England, near Canterbury, were facing their first questions relating to living together in religious diversity. Without any real thought about the implications, the community had welcomed as an assistant a Canadian Roman Catholic priest on a sabbatical year. He wished to celebrate the eucharist each day and we were glad of this but what about our people with mental handicaps, who belonged to the Church of England? Surely they – and those assistants who were also members of that church – could be offered communion? After all, they would have to go ten miles into Canterbury for a weekday eucharist.

The Roman Catholic ecumenist we consulted asked the right question: How could we best help those with mental handicaps to belong to their own church? The advice of this priest who was well-versed in ecumenical matters encouraged us to use our heads as well as our rather naive hearts.

We reached the painful decision to obey the rules of the Roman Catholic Church, but not everyone agreed with that decision. We decided to have a weekday community eucharist once a week during the working day – Anglican one week, Roman Catholic the next. On other weekdays our priest-assistant would celebrate the eucharist at seven in the morning, before the start of the community day. Perhaps the most important aspect of this decision was the fact that we contacted the local Anglican rector, who celebrated the fortnightly Anglican eucharist in the community and thus became involved with our people who belonged to his church.

Thus at the start of the first community in the U.K. we confronted the reality of division at the eucharist and faced the irreconcilable rules of our different churches. Specifically, in the context of the U.K., the main difference lies in the canon law of the Roman Catholic Church, which does not normally allow members of most other churches to receive communion at its eucharist, nor does it permit its own members to receive communion at the eucharist of most other churches. The rules stem from a particular view of the nature or the church and the view that sharing in the eucharist, generally speaking, must be a sign of unity achieved, although it is recognized that it can also be a means to Christian unity. The Roman Catholic Church is concerned that the seriousness of divisions, which have their origins in differences of belief, be appropriately emphasized. The Anglican communion, on the other hand, welcomes confirmed members of other churches to its eucharist and permits its members to receive the eucharist of other denominations, particularly in situations where Christians from different churches are living together and working to promote unity.

Inevitably the "rules" made assistants angry and our people with mental handicaps did not understand why they sometimes could not receive communion at the eucharist. In such situations it is easy to bring the feelings surrounding the divisions at the eucharist, such as anger and incomprehension, into our relationships with each other, and this we undoubtedly did.

Ecumenism frequently subsists in the development of friendship and trust between people. In other words, the barriers to unity arising from difficulties in human relationships and cultural differences can be much more substantial than those arising from actual differences in teaching and belief.

In the early days of l'Arche Lambeth in London, Doris, who was then in her fifties, showed us that broken relationships between churches and their individual members frequently have more to do with insensitivity than with doctrine. Doris has a mental handicap and is paralysed down one side of her body. She is a strong-minded woman who had survived nearly half a century of hospital life before coming to l'Arche. She remains resilient and full of life, though she still retains considerable anger. Doris did not always know where to focus that anger and we were not always sensitive to her fears and wounds. She particularly disliked having her paralysed hand held. One night at prayers when we joined hands to say the "Our Father," a new assistant who had not been warned tried to take Doris' hand. She was too insistent, and Doris became angry and stamped out, shouting, "I don't like the way you Catholics pray." The anger was right and we were at fault for not having warned the assistant, but the focus was wrong in that the "problem" clearly had nothing to do with the way in which Catholics pray.

The ecumenical vocation of l'Arche unfolded gradually and with many difficulties through the presence in our communities of men and women with mental handicaps who belong to different Christian traditions and Faiths. These have been from the start "the core members" – those at the heart, the centre of the communities. In respecting and valuing them, we obviously respect and value their stories, their membership of a particular family – though many no longer possess family ties – and their affiliation to a religious tradition or a particular Christian church. Respect for an individual implies respect for that person's church or religious faith and a desire to know and love that human institution, limited like ourselves by human frailty, but nonetheless part of the fragmented religious dimension of humanity in which Christians perceive the broken body of Christ.

2

Following the signs

The impact of our unity within diversity is perhaps greatest in Holy Week. To take the Lambeth community as an example: on Maundy Thursday, those who live in each community household, or are "attached" while living elsewhere, gather to wash one another's feet. This is usually done in small groups and in ways that are simple and solemn. Simple words are sung, Chapter 13 of John's Gospel is read and the washing and anointing of one another's feet begins in silence. It takes time, because it is carried out slowly and thoroughly, with great gentleness and tenderness.

The washing of the feet has acquired deep significance for all our communities and is increasingly used at solemn moments.

On Maundy Thursday we follow this ceremony with a simple version of a Passover meal, remembering the history of the people of Israel and valuing it as part of our history. Many of us then go to services in our different parishes.

On the morning of Good Friday we gather to walk silently through the neighbourhood, carrying a large cross, a crown of thorns and a purple robe. As we come to each community house or workshop, those who live or work there enact part of the passion of Jesus, a different person therefore taking the part of Jesus at each house and wearing the purple robe and crown of thorns. Participation as a community in these two or three hours each year has imprinted the story of Jesus' passion upon us in a way that is beyond words. It is a living and *feeling* way of recognizing that we are part of the body of Christ. Most of us know something of the suffering history of people in the community, both

*The meeting between Jesus and his mother enacted
by members of l'Arche Lambeth*

those with mental handicaps and assistants, and it is moving to
see this incorporated consciously or unconsciously into the suffering of Jesus.

On the afternoon of Good Friday many of us go once more
to our different parish churches, carrying into the more formal
setting the impact and feeling of the morning.

In the evening after supper we gather to spend time – about
an hour – around the same cross we carried in the morning which
is now laid on the ground. The room is dimly lit by candles, three
of which are near the cross. One or two people witness to the
place of the cross in their lives, either verbally or through draw-
ings or mime. Then in silence, interspersed with quiet singing of
"Jesus remember me when you come into your kingdom" and
"Adoremus te, Domine," we sit around the cross into which
someone drives three nails, that sound expressing and echoing

the pain of those who have just witnessed to the place of the cross in their lives at the start of our time together.

After a while people start coming towards the cross to touch it or kiss it. Some place their heads against it, staying there in silence for a few moments. This is a time of mysterious union between pain and peace, suffering and healing, the reality of which escapes us most of the time. It demonstrates the full meaning of the statement that l'Arche is built on suffering, and the slow process of healing which can take place there for many people, whether mentally handicapped or assistant.

It is an intense experience, an insight into the meaning of life and particularly of the lives of those with mental handicaps who live at the level of their hearts.

In many ways our daily life can be intense, and much of that intensity relates to the painful experiences of our people and the way in which these resonate with our own, frequently less dramatic experiences. It is valuable to take stock of this quietly, on the anniversary of the day on which Christ died.

After this time together on the night of Good Friday, the cross is moved into a small prayer room and lamps are laid along the vertical and horizontal bars, where Christ's body would have hung. Those who come to spend a time of vigil now see these lights as an unmistakable sign of new life: resurrection at the point of death.

On Saturday night or Easter Sunday morning we again go to our different churches and join the parish celebrations. We come together once more as a community early on Sunday afternoon to celebrate the resurrection – Jesus alive. The cross is now decked with flowers, the meeting of Jesus with Mary Magdalen is enacted, and there is singing and dancing. The contrast between the night of Good Friday and the celebration of Easter day was highlighted on one occasion by Paul, and illustrates the capacity of our people to live the death-resurrection cycle. On Good Friday Paul had played the part of Jesus as we reached his community house. Here, as Jesus he was crucified, died and was "buried." On Easter morning Paul came down dressed in his best suit, wearing his red bow tie. He felt that preparations were taking rather too long and went into the garden, to the spot of his

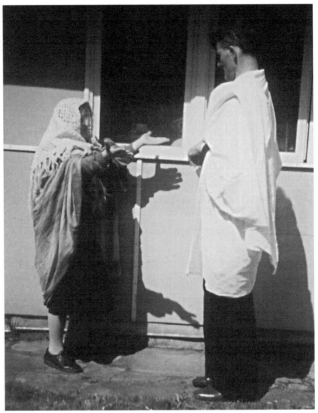

*The meeting between Jesus and Mary Magdalen
enacted by members of l'Arche Lambeth*

Friday "burial." Here he shouted at the top of his voice: "Hurry up, can't you see that I'm alive?"

Domestic liturgies

In 1992 the l'Arche Commission on Ecumenism for North America, using material from the communities in Canada and the United States, brought out a wonderful collection of domestic liturgies[8] which covered the Christian year, birthdays, anniversa-

---

8   Examples of domestic liturgies from a number of communities are given in the Appendix.

ries and other special events and occasions. Tom Ryan, Director of the Canadian Centre for Ecumenism in Montreal, wrote in the Foreword:

> What has always been true is even more true now: what we have in common weighs much more heavily in the balance than anything that divides us. This reality must be clearly witnessed to at the local level and take hold in the way Christians perceive and relate to one another....
>
> The communities of l'Arche are leading the way into the future. The mantle of leadership comes to rest upon your shoulders all unsought. In opening up and unpacking the calling God has given to you, you have discovered it to be an ecumenical one, rich with implications for the whole church.... You come from different traditions of practice in the faith, so you are obliged to look for ways of sharing faith in the context of your common life....

As we have seen, in countries such as France the great majority of people are, at least nominally, Roman Catholic, and church membership within our communities therefore reflects this. However, in the larger French communities there are nearly always a small number of assistants who are Protestant and, increasingly, assistants who are members of the Orthodox churches. Occasionally within such communities there may be people with handicaps who are Protestant or belong to other Faiths.

These larger communities frequently act as host to assistants of other denominations who come together for gatherings such as retreats. Thus they have some experience of struggling to meet the needs of people from different churches, and occasionally of different Faiths.

It is, however, the interdenominational communities in countries such as Germany, Switzerland, the U.K., North America and Australia, which continue to struggle with the whole question of how to express our unity as Christians belonging to different churches, while ensuring that we are active members of these churches at a local level. This is complicated

Alia Qureshi of the Daybreak community with her father,
who helps the community to deepen their understanding
of Muslim prayer and spirituality

by the presence of assistants and a few people with handicaps who either wish to be Christian but without church affiliation, or else have a spirituality with no explicit foundation in any of the main world religions.

Most members of the Daybreak community near Toronto belong to Anglican, Roman Catholic or United churches; however, both Judaism and the Faith of Islam are represented among those with mental handicaps. Because of these representatives, everyone has the opportunity to deepen their understanding of these other Faiths. At the time of Ellen's Bat Mitzvah,[9] Beth Porter wrote: "Ellen was called up to the Torah for the first time and said the Hebrew blessings before and after the Torah reading.... Ellen's joy and ease were very evident and quite contagious. As we prayed and sang and danced and ate together, we sensed again the gift and grace of l'Arche – the gift of the core person who breaks down barriers and draws people together in creative and energizing ways that can change our world for the better." Ellen's parents preside each year at a Seder Passover meal in the community.

Attitudes and practices first introduced in the Roman Catholic Trosly community became traditions which were adopted and developed in interdenominational communities, and, indeed, in inter-faith communities.

In Trosly people with mental handicaps have always participated fully in the eucharistic celebrations, and ways were found to prepare non-verbal people to receive the sacraments. Evening prayers in community households were simple and humanly "warm." People sat round the meal table or fireside, held hands, and had the focus of a candle and perhaps another symbol, as well as simple pictures of gospel scenes.

The life of every community household was punctuated by birthdays, anniversaries, and celebrations to mark arrivals and departures as well as death and burial.

The transmission of these traditions into new communities has led to the development of domestic liturgies. This has been

---

9   Bat/Bar Mitzvah: literally, "Daughter/Son of the Commandments" – a celebration
     somewhat akin to confirmation in the Christian tradition.

*Ellen Weinstein of l'Arche Daybreak holding the Torah scroll
after the celebration of her Bat Mitzvah*

particularly marked in interdenominational communities, in which we are obliged to attend different church services, where these liturgies meet our urgent need to worship together.

In terms of unity among Christians, the importance of community liturgies lies in the ways in which hearts are touched and people are drawn together. Connections are made between their own feelings and experiences, or those of others, and the experience and feelings of Jesus as recounted in the Gospels. In other words, liturgy and daily life and experience become a single entity.

In some instances such liturgies meet profound human needs common to all: the need for affirmation, belonging, forgiveness and solidarity. Thus we are attempting to build friendship and deepen trust.

The prayer of l'Arche

This prayer, which was said or sung every evening in the first little community house in Trosly, was first addressed to Mary, asking her to help us to open the doors of our houses and our hearts to the poor and to see, in our suffering and broken brothers and sisters, the living presence of Jesus. The community then turned to the Lord, asking him to bless and smile on us through the poor.

The prayer altered as communities spread to North America, India, U.K., Africa, and Australia. It was subsequently addressed to God our Father, but the several variations included the plea that the Lord bless and smile on us through "the poor," although expressed in a variety of ways.

Lord, through the hands of your little ones we ask you to bless us; through the eyes of those who are rejected, we ask you to smile on us.

When we showed our new English version of the prayer to a priest in the U.K. in 1973, he remarked after a rapid reading: "Have you got the roles reversed in this bit about blessing and smiling? Shouldn't you be asking the Lord to bless and smile on the poor through you?" Chapter Twenty-five of Matthew's Gospel certainly puts the accent on "doing for" rather than

L'Arche Lambeth on pilgrimage from London to Canterbury

"receiving from" people in need: ". . . for I was hungry and you gave me food, I was thirsty and you gave me drink. I was a stranger and you welcomed me." Yet we all have something to give. The concept of "unlikely givers" is still particularly difficult for many people who are asked to recognize the gifts of those with mental handicaps.

I remember that the original U.K. version of the prayer of l'Arche, written when we were preparing the first community near Canterbury in 1973, brought in Mary somewhat discreetly half-way through the prayer because we felt that a prayer *addressed* principally to Mary would not be appropriate in a country where devotion to the Mother of God was not part of their Christian tradition for large numbers of people. At the same time we did not want to lose the link with the original French version. So part of our prayer read: "Mary, Mother of Jesus, give us greatness of heart that we may welcome all those you send." When the second community was envisaged in Inverness, our "first draft" became "Spirit of God, give us greatness of heart...," and thus it has remained for the U.K. communities.

Retreats and pilgrimages

In the very early days, retreats in l'Arche were unmistakably in the Roman Catholic tradition as were the regular pilgrimages to Lourdes. As l'Arche spread beyond France, the organizers of retreats endeavoured to make them ecumenical, and in 1974 Ann and Steve Newroth and others organized an amazing pilgrimage from l'Arche and Faith and Light in Canada and the U.S.A. to Canterbury Cathedral and then to Taizé. The participation of over two hundred pilgrims, half of whom had mental handicaps, in the sung eucharist on Easter Sunday is still remembered in Canterbury. Many people were deeply touched by the event, including the Archbishop of Canterbury, Michael Ramsey, and we acquired many new friends as a result.[10]

The ways in which retreats and pilgrimages became ecumenical varied from one continent to another. Some organizers had access to advice and guidelines from previous gatherings; others were starting from scratch. In 1992 the l'Arche Commission on

---

[10] *An Ecumenical Journey: L'Arche in the U.K.*

Ecumenism (Europe) produced guidelines[11] based on experiences in France and the U.K. where retreats had brought together Roman Catholics from France and Belgium, Protestants from Germany and Switzerland, Anglicans from the U.K., and various other people. These guidelines were compiled to help the organizers, who were almost always Roman Catholic, to plan interdenominational retreats. They summarized current "best practice" for

1. *Retreats with a Roman Catholic basis*, likely to take place in France or Belgium, which included individuals of other denominations if they so wished. Here the principal recommendations related to the need to obtain permission from the local Roman Catholic bishop for eucharistic hospitality to be offered on a particular "one-off" occasion. A special non-eucharistic service was also recommended in order to celebrate and affirm the diversity of traditions represented and organizers were reminded that sensitivity and human warmth were particularly important.

2. *Interdenominational retreats*, usually in the U.K. but increasingly in other European countries, which should be planned by a group representing each of the traditions to which participants belonged. There would be a celebration of the eucharist in different traditions on different days, greater emphasis on the Word of God in scripture than would be the case in specifically Roman Catholic gatherings, and the possibility of two places in which to pray – one with the reserved sacrament and the other containing a Bible, a plain cross and perhaps an icon. There were marked sensitivities around the question of the prayer room, because Roman Catholics, particularly those from predominantly Catholic countries, valued the possibility of praying before the reserved sacrament, preferably exposed on the altar. Protestants, especially those from Germany, found this concept alien. For this reason it was finally decided that there should be two separate places in which to pray.

---

[11]   *Guidelines on Organizing Retreats.*

In December 1993 the Commission on Ecumenism (Europe) produced a brief paper by Donald Allchin, *The Reservation of the Blessed Sacrament*, in which he explains the position of the different churches regarding such reservation and the possible attitudes of members of those churches to the concept of reservation. The final paragraph reads:

> Where there is mutual confidence and good will and a certain degree of mutual understanding, where there is sensitivity to the feelings and traditions of others, it need not be impossible to find a way through this apparent impasse. Where the place of the eucharistic presence is linked with other symbols of the Word, for instance an open Bible, or a familiar icon, it seems possible that we shall be able to come together in a more united way for silent personal prayer as well as in the celebration of the liturgy. But such unity will have to be worked for, it cannot be taken for granted.[12]

Covenant retreats

Covenant retreats provide an opportunity for assistants to affirm the commitment or covenant to which they feel called within l'Arche. Those who wish are invited to respond individually to the question: "You are invited to live a covenant in l'Arche with Jesus and all your brothers and sisters, especially the poorest and the weakest. Do you want this?" In Roman Catholic retreats the commitment has been made just before the distribution of communion at the eucharist on the final day.

When Anglican and Protestant assistants wished to announce their covenant with l'Arche, we had to decide how to celebrate our commitment *together* in a situation where there was division at the eucharist.

A group in the U.K. developed a liturgy during which people renewed their baptismal vows, then announced their covenant. This was followed by a solemn washing of each other's feet, the whole liturgy being carried out in the context of the account of the washing of the feet in Chapter 13 of John's Gospel.

---

[12]   *The Reservation of the Blessed Sacrament*, p. 5.

The Oratory at l'Arche Trosly-Breuil

This liturgy was subsequently modified in order to accommodate Hindu members of l'Arche. Instead of the renewal of baptismal vows, Hindu members renewed their Faith as follows: "We renounce evil; we believe and trust in God." After the singing of

> From unreality lead us to the Real,
> From darkness lead us to Light,
> From death lead us to Immortality,

there was a reading from the writings of Vivekananda, a Hindu holy man. The question preceding the announcement of the covenant was adjusted as follows: "You are invited to live a covenant of love in l'Arche with your brothers and sisters, especially the poorest and the weakest. Do you want this?"[13]

Prayer and places in which to pray

A time and a place in which to pray are vital for most assistants and many people with handicaps within l'Arche. Prayer is very simple for us and, although the symbols may vary according to local culture, religious affiliation or tradition, a lighted candle or oil lamp is unlikely to be absent.

In most communities there is at least one chapel, oratory or prayer room. These vary in size and in precise use: some are mainly for celebration of the eucharist and community prayer; others are primarily for private, silent, meditative, and contemplative prayer. In the first community of Trosly there is a large chapel, but also a small oratory, where the blessed sacrament is reserved and exposed regularly. This has been a precious place of prayer, not only for many people with handicaps, but for countless assistants and an endless stream of visitors. As happens in such places, one *feels* the prayer that has been offered there: As T. S. Eliot wrote in *Little Gidding:* "You are here to kneel / Here prayer has been valid." Despite the strongly Roman Catholic ethos in which the sacrament is exposed, many people of other traditions and other Faiths come to pray in the oratory.

The symbolic focus for prayer is clearly very important. The International Council of l'Arche has suggested that Christian communities might consider having three symbols in their places of prayer: the Bible, an icon and the reserved sacrament. This is not as simple an option as it might appear at first sight. Many communities, including those which have made a formal statement of their Christian and interdenominational identity, have yet to deal with such matters as the symbolic focus in the prayer room because of the individual sensitivities involved.

In the tiny prayer room within the Lambeth community there is an open Bible, an icon of the Virgin and Child, of Christ, or of the Trinity, depending on the liturgical season. And there is a large bowl with a towel. The latter has become a most

---

13   *The Covenant,* January 1989, International Office, L'Arche, BP 35, 60350 Trosly Breuil, France.

Prayer room in Calcutta community

important symbol for l'Arche in the U.K., as it represents Jesus washing the feet of his disciples on the night before he died.

In India in 1983 Chris Sadler wrote a long and thoughtful paper entitled "The Spiritual Vocation of l'Arche in India," in which she expresses concern about some aspects of Christian "domination," both real and apparent. At the time the great majority of l'Arche assistants in India were Roman Catholics from Western countries, and the question had been raised about celebration of the eucharist and reservation of the sacrament in places for quiet prayer.

> Here perhaps more than anywhere exists the tension between individual needs which are deep and sincere, and respect for the sensitivities of others. While we are certainly not trying to make a new "all-inclusive" religion, would we be happy to see the "compounds" of our communities dotted about with various little Temples, Catholic and Protestant chapels, a Mosque? That is the logical implication of having a chapel of adoration with the reserved sacrament....
>
> Through mistakes and growing awareness of our insensitivities we have discovered how much the celebration of the Eucharist, which is so essential a part of some of our lives, has to remain discreet, and if possible outside the "programme" of our community life together, whether at home or in our larger gatherings or special celebrations. Slowly we are learning that there must be a willingness to sacrifice even one's spiritual needs, unless they are wholly inspired by a greater sacrifice of love.

Chris went to see Bede Griffiths[14] in order to ask his advice on what she had written. His comment was: "Chris, I have nothing to say. You are living it; we are still talking about it."

In one of his early books, Bede Griffiths gave an indication of how he saw his own task: "The task was not so much to bring

---

[14]   Bede Griffiths, a Benedictine monk from England, came to India in 1955. In 1983 he was living in the Saccidananda Ashram in Tamil Nadu, which was a pioneering attempt to found a Christian community in India which would incorporate the customs of a Hindu Ashram and the traditional forms of Indian life and thought. He died in 1993.

The seven sacred books in the garden prayer room in Calcutta

Christ to India as to discover Christ already present and active in the Hindu soul. We can say that the mystery of Christ is hidden in all religion as it was hidden in Judaism and that Christ himself comes to reveal this hidden meaning, to make clear what was obscure, to make explicit what was implicit, to perfect what was imperfect."

Today, much of the high tension of which Chris writes has disappeared. Time and increasing sensitivity have played their part and the help given to the Asha Niketan communities by Indian Christians has been of the greatest value. So many of them are also steeped in Hinduism and therefore able to interpret the cultural context of the expressions of different religions.

At the start of Asha Niketan in Kerala, South India, there were Hindus, Muslims and Christians in the community. Muslims do not have images of any kind in their places of worship, whereas for a Hindu, who has such a profound sense of God in all creation, every flower and stone and lamp can become the focal point of worship. Chris, who founded the community, asked the Muslim members if the place of prayer could have a light in the centre, and this was agreed. The oil lamp was placed on some stones upon which one could also put flowers. Viswanathan, who was a much valued member of the community and had a mental handicap, was a Hindu. One day he was sitting at the entrance of the place of prayer when a passer-by looking in saw the stones and the flowers and turning to him, asked: "Which god do you pray to?" Viswanathan replied: "Which god? . . . I do not know which God.... We pray in the Light, that is all."

In the Calcutta community in North India the first room one sees upon entering the house is the prayer room in which the community meets morning and evening. In it there is a wall hanging which bears the symbols of the seven major religions of India. Just beyond is the room in which people gather to eat. Outside in the grounds is a small building reserved for silent prayer where the sacred books of the seven major religions of India are kept, each wrapped in precious silk and placed in a separate niche in the wall. Every day sees a different book placed at the centre of the room – the focus for the day. At the same time the remaining books are each moved forward so that they come to the centre in rotation. It has been said that when approaching another Faith one should take one's shoes off, because God has been there first....

In a number of countries, both East and West, inter-faith initiatives are recognizing and affirming the beliefs of different World Faiths and developing relations of mutual trust, while undertaking research and maintaining dialogue at a deep level. In the U.K., for example, the Roman Catholic Diocese of Westminster has a long-standing inter-faith programme which facilitates a learning process and provides the opportunity to develop friendships and share in prayer.

In October 1986, John Paul II invited the heads and representatives of Christian churches and ecclesial communities and of World Religions to gather with him in Assisi to pray for peace. In addition to the many representing different Christian churches and the Jewish delegations, the Dalai Lama came with other representatives of Buddhism, as well as representatives of Hinduism, Islam, Jainism, Shinto, Sikhism, Traditional religions and Zoroastrianism.

In the course of his several addresses,[15] the Pope said:

> For the first time in human history, Christian churches and religions from all parts of the world gathered in the same place to show that peace is an imperative for the conscience of believers who are seeking truth about God, about our destiny, about the history of humanity....
>
> I have chosen this town of Assisi as the place for our Day of Prayer for Peace because of the particular significance of the holy man venerated here – Saint Francis – known and revered by so many throughout the world as a symbol of peace, reconciliation and brotherhood.

He reminded his listeners that "Francis had discovered the value of poverty, the value of a simple and austere life, in imitation of Jesus Christ whom he intended to serve." Francis was indeed a man with a passion for poverty, and had chosen *poverty* as the path to reconciliation and peace.

Evening prayer

In India there is a tradition of morning and evening prayer and in the communities of Asha Niketan this tradition is strongly maintained.

Chris writes of the Kerala community, situated on ten acres of rocky hillside in South India, which needs its own source of water: "The first well which was fifty feet deep and ten feet across, was excavated with extreme difficulty and when it became necessary to build a second well this proved an even

---

[15] *Assisi, World Day of Prayer for Peace, 27 October 1986,* Pontifical Commission "Justitia et Pax," 1987 (Pontifical Council for Justice and Peace, Piazza St. Calisto 16, 00153, Rome, Italy).

longer and more difficult task. We almost abandoned it several times, and the day we finally reached the source of water in the deep rock-bedded well, I suggested that we all drink some of this water during evening prayer. I was completely unprepared for the effect on me of the litany which sprang from Viswanathan's own deep source. He sang for perhaps ten minutes, repeating over and over: 'O God, O God, you have given water, sweet water, new water in the new well.'" Chris had a sense of deep unity in the group brought about by this outpouring of praise from Viswanathan. "He taught us about wonder and thanksgiving. He also taught us about hospitality and not taking ourselves too seriously."

Kunhikanaran, the present leader of the Kerala community, is a Hindu who writes of spiritual growth taking place in himself and of the essence of Hindu spirituality, discovered at evening prayer: "Lancelot prayed in the name of Jesus, Ramesh in the name of Krishna, Zakaria in the name of Allah: personal prayers were accompanied by songs of different religions. At the end everyone said the Asha Niketan prayer. After some moments of silence and with radiant faces we all gave *Shanti* – peace – to each other."

Ravi in Asha Niketan Bangalore very often sings a particular *bahjan*, Hazel Bradley remembers:

Krishna, jaya, jaya,
Krishna, jaya, jaya,
Krishna, jaya, jaya, namor, namor,

in praise of Krishna; Ravi is Hindu. Then he sings:

Christa, jaya, jaya
Christa, jaya, jaya
Christa, jaya, jaya, namor, namor

in praise of Christ and then he concludes with:

Jyoti, jaya, jaya
Jyoti, jaya, jaya
Jyoti, jaya, jaya, namor, namor

in praise of the Light *(jyoti)* which unites us all.

31

Within l'Arche communities in the West the tradition of evening prayer is not necessarily so strongly maintained. There is great variation from one community to another and, within a particular community, from one household to another. There are many reasons why the tradition of evening prayer may lapse, but there is no doubt that the households which maintain a tradition of regular evening prayer regard it as precious and valuable.

Prayer is also associated with the meal. It may take place before the meal or afterwards while still sitting at the table. Some may choose to come together to pray after the washing up. Members with handicaps pray for their families, sometimes giving long lists of names.... They need to *belong* to that family in spite of family experiences which have not always been positive. Then there is the naming of friends, relations or others who are ill, in hospital, or in difficulties, and those who have died and their families are remembered; sometimes there is a moving and astonishing humility: "O God, please help me to accept to be what I am." The man who spoke those words in one of the French communities was both physically and mentally disabled. He was often angry and aggressive in trying to overcome his handicap, yet, like the publican in the parable, he was prepared to acknowledge his vulnerability and his need for help. As the prayer group broke up, several people came to him and thanked him for his prayer saying how much it had helped them. In his weakness others found strength and he had been affirmed. This small incident reveals the power of weakness and vulnerability to draw people to each other and provide an opportunity to transform relationships.

3

Relationships between l'Arche and the churches

Père Thomas Philippe had a great love for the church, as well as a sense of the vital place of the poor within it. He and Jean Vanier therefore developed close links with their local Roman Catholic bishop, to the extent that, over the years, Bishop Stephane Desmazières of the Diocese of Beauvais and his successor Bishop Adolphe-Marie Hardy took the unusual step of ordaining three priests specifically for l'Arche. Local bishops in France and throughout the world have also authorized members of the clergy as well as lay people to act as pastoral ministers to specific communities, usually on a part-time basis.

Similar contacts with local bishops have been encouraged as new communities opened, and these contacts have become more complex in the case of interdenominational communities.

The ability of l'Arche to make and maintain such contacts has necessarily varied and matters are not improved by the fact that the leaders of communities are overburdened and struggle to establish priorities, while bishops and the leaders of other churches find themselves in a similar situation.

There is now a greater acceptance and understanding of the interdenominational and inter-faith nature of l'Arche, both within our own communities and in the wider world. However, the fact that l'Arche International does not "belong" to a particular church can raise questions for the parish clergy and church leaders of all denominations in the vicinity of communities which are Christian and wish to be integrated within their local churches. To whom are individual communities accountable, and within which church?

Religious affiliation and identity

Each community of l'Arche is obviously part of the locality in which it finds itself and members not only belong to the community, but usually to a particular family as well as to a church, temple, mosque or synagogue. They may have an occupation or profession and belong to a particular organization or club. While the "belonging" in the widest sense is a key element within l'Arche, the majority of men and women with a mental handicap arrive in the community with little if any sense of belonging to any organization or structure. One of the important factors in the creation of community is the discovery or rediscovery of "belonging."

Religious belonging is clearly an essential element for the community and consequently for the individuals within it. In determining such belonging, communities are asked to take into account the following:

1. The history of the community, including any specific intentions of the founders.
2. The present church or religious membership of community members, particularly those with mental handicaps.
3. The present sources of nourishment for the religious and spiritual life of the community, which may pertain to one or more Christian traditions or to differing World Faiths.

A community may be:

1. Of one Faith, and, if Christian,
   a) part of a particular Christian church or tradition (at present, those rooted in the Roman Catholic Church predominate, mainly in France or Belgium);
   b) interdenominational.
2. Inter-faith.

Communities are beginning to define their religious identity and although there is sometimes an understandable reluctance to do this for fear of "excluding" people, the existing community and potential new members need to be able to identify and clarify their expectations of one another. The definition of religious identity is essential, too, if we are to dialogue with local bishops and other church and religious leaders. If they are to relate to us they need to know who we are!

The definition of identity also ensures that the community continues to be sustained appropriately and we must recognize that the religious identity of a community may change over the years as new people come and the question of identity therefore needs to be reviewed at appropriate intervals.

For some communities the definition of religious identity has to take particular account of considerations other than the religious affiliation of the members with mental handicaps. Elizabeth Hunter, Zone coordinator for Africa, writes:

> The l'Arche communities in Ouagadougou (Burkina Faso) and Bouaké (Ivory Coast) have defined their religious identity as Roman Catholic *and* open to people of all religions. This decision was taken because the majority of committed assistants (African or from Western countries) are Roman Catholic and there are particular links with that church.
>
> Locally there are no significant links between the different Christian churches or between differing World Faiths, and there is little or no dialogue at these levels.
>
> The children we welcome to the community come because of their human needs and regardless of any religious affiliation. We also support and care for children living in their families and the families have no hesitation in working with us because they know that our particular religious identity has no bearing on who we help.
>
> In general, in our part of West Africa people of different religions live peacefully alongside each other and within one family one not infrequently finds members of different religions. The ease with which local people live alongside each other helps us. We ask Muslim and Animist families if their handicapped children may join in our times of prayer. Usually they are happy to allow this. But we are particularly careful about the children who live in the community and have no family. In Ouagadougou, when we pray in the evening, Ali who is Muslim and is handicapped goes to pray with our watchman who is also Muslim.

We constantly seek ways in which to come to terms with our different backgrounds and this includes dialogue with religious leaders: priests, pastors, imams (Muslim). There is a long way to go simply in terms of acceptance of the person with a handicap. For instance there is still difficulty in allowing Roman Catholics with mental handicaps to receive communion in the Roman Catholic parish.

We *are* living something prophetic in the sense that it is people with mental handicaps who draw very different people (parents, friends, committees, religious leaders) into dialogue regardless of religious affiliation.

Accompanying bishops and other church leaders

As l'Arche developed, the International Council sought to invite a particular Roman Catholic bishop, in a country where communities belonged to that church, to "accompany" those communities, listening to their experience, advising them, and facilitating their contacts with other local bishops. Since 1986 the bishop who accompanies the French communities has made it possible for the l'Arche Zone Coordinator, Odile Ceyrac, the Pastoral Minister for the Zone, Gilbert Adam, and Jean Vanier to meet annually with the bishops who have a community of l'Arche in their diocese, during the General Assembly of French bishops.

It has been less easy to obtain the appointment of accompanying bishops and other church leaders in countries such as Canada, the U.S.A., and Germany, where interdenominational communities predominate, because of the need to involve church leaders of different denominations. Though similar conditions could be found in the U.K., it was easier there, for two reasons. The first was the emergence in 1986 of a small group of two Anglican bishops and a Roman Catholic bishop who knew the l'Arche communities in Kent, London and Liverpool. In 1995 the group included a representative of the Free Church Federal Council (which brings together Baptists, Methodists, United Reformed and other independent and Afro-Caribbean churches), and a representative of the Church of Scotland. These accompanying church leaders meet twice a year with the U.K. Regional Coordinators, the chairperson of the Pastoral Ecumenical Committee of l'Arche U.K. and a member of the National Committee of l'Arche in the U.K.

The second reason why ongoing dialogue with church leaders has been comparatively easy to establish in the U.K. is the formal existence since 1987 of an inter-church process, "Not Strangers but Pilgrims," which links virtually all the Christian churches in the U.K. The ecumenical dimension of l'Arche communities has ensured that substantial bonds have been forged between ourselves and those involved in the inter-church process, hopefully to the benefit of both sides. The close association between l'Arche U.K. and the accompanying church leaders and between l'Arche and those involved in the inter-church process is, in both cases, rooted in friendship and trust which are such key factors in the establishment of ecumenical dialogue.

International level

Almost from the beginning of l'Arche, Jean Vanier has met regularly with the Pontifical Council for the Promotion of Christian Unity and with the Pontifical Council for Inter-Religious Dialogue in Rome. The International Coordinator of l'Arche also attends these meetings. In 1995 Jean was invited to give a paper on the vision of l'Arche in terms of working with people of non-Christian religions to the general assembly of some forty bishops (mainly from Asia) who advise the Pontifical Council for Inter-Religious Dialogue.

More recently Jean and the International Coordinator have met with the Archbishop of Canterbury, the Primate of the Anglican communion, in London and with the Secretary General of the World Council of Churches in Geneva. The purpose of such meetings is to convey the nature, spirituality and ecumenical commitment of l'Arche communities, stressing particularly the place of those with mental handicaps in the divided Christian Church. They are also a forum in which to express our wish to be questioned and challenged by the churches as part of the process of accountability, and in order to develop and clarify our thinking.

Meetings also take place with the Pontifical Council for the Laity, and in the early days there was a certain tension between l'Arche and the Council over the question of "belonging" to the

Roman Catholic Church in terms of receiving a legal or canonical status. Yet it was clear that the question of our "belonging" not only transcended denominational barriers but went beyond the "limits" of World Faiths, simply because communities welcomed people with handicaps regardless of religious affiliation (or the lack of it) and that these people were the core members. Legal or canonical status within the Roman Catholic Church was therefore inappropriate, because of the necessary implication of any such canonical definition that l'Arche was *primarily* Roman Catholic.

Tension remains, however, for a number of Roman Catholic members of l'Arche within communities belonging to that church who feel a deep need to receive a blessing or some other form of affirmation from their church as an expression of their long-term commitment to l'Arche. Respect for their needs has led to establishment of appropriate ways in which such commitments may be recognized by the church: for example a commitment to the celibate life (perhaps for a limited term) may be expressed in an appropriate way to a bishop or priest. The possibility of making such a commitment is not of course restricted to members of the Roman Catholic Church.

The role of the International Council and Commissions on Ecumenism

Every two years the executive of the International Council of l'Arche meets with church leaders from a number of countries, leaders who accompany our communities, and in 1990 the Council issued a paper entitled "The Place of Ecumenism in l'Arche" (revised and reissued in 1994).[16] This paper stressed the ecumenical vocation of the communities and outlined the vision of l'Arche in terms of ecumenism and detailed the considerations which must be taken into account if we are to clarify and develop our ecumenical approach. The International Council is very much aware of widely differing experiences and attitudes within the communities world-wide and takes the view that "ecumenical problems" cannot be solved centrally. It therefore seeks to

---

[16]   *Ecumenism in l'Arche* (1).

encourage individual communities to work closely with local churches and particularly with local bishops and church leaders.

In 1986 and 1987 the International Council appointed three Commissions on Ecumenism (each one to work within the particular geographical areas covered by the three Zones of the Federation) in order to deepen reflection on this aspect of the lives of communities. The mandates of the Commissions were renewed by the International Council in 1991.

Europe – Africa – Middle East Zone

The members were principally Roman Catholic (reflecting membership of the communities at the time) and came from Belgium, France, Switzerland, and the U.K. A long and detailed questionnaire was sent to the thirty-six communities (thirty-three in Europe, two in Africa and one on the West Bank). All but three of the European communities responded and a comprehensive analysis of the responses was sent to the International Council. The Commission subsequently tried to respond to the most frequently expressed concerns and questions raised by communities and over several years a number of guidelines and reflection papers were produced.[17]

In writing these papers we drew on our experiences as members or associates of Roman Catholic and interdenominational communities and were immensely helped by Donald Allchin, who has known l'Arche for many years and is a theologian of long experience in ecumenical dialogue. During the first Commission on Ecumenism (1987-1991) we also consulted a Swiss Protestant pastor who was in close touch with the interdenominational l'Arche community in that country. During the second Commission (1991-1993) we also benefited from the presence of Pastor Schneider and subsequently Sister Hélène, both of the Swiss Protestant church, and Gérard Daucourt, a Roman Catholic bishop.

With the inter-faith situations of the West Bank and two African communities we found ourselves out of our depth. The questions raised concerning interdenominational aspects of life in communities in Africa and on the West Bank were necessarily

---

17   See the Bibliography.

linked to relationships between Christian churches in the countries concerned, and we were not sufficiently *au fait* with these.

The necessary sensitivity of assistants finding themselves in complex inter-faith situations is illustrated by the fact that a member of the West Bank community was a very severely disabled Muslim girl who did not speak. It was noticed, however, that during Christian prayer times she would try to sing "alleluia" with the others, and the assistants were concerned for her because they knew that the word was not part of her Islamic faith.

To a limited extent we were able to obtain appropriate guidance for them, but because of our overall inability to offer the required assistance to communities in Africa and the Middle East, we recommended that the Federation take the necessary steps to find more local guidance in ecumenical matters.

Because of the widely differing ecumenical situations in different countries we also recommended to the International Council the formation of national Pastoral Ecumenical Committees in European countries where there were a number of l'Arche communities. These committees would need to draw support and develop agendas in consultation with national ecumenical bodies. They would also have to consider the needs and what was realistically possible for l'Arche communities in the countries concerned. In the event, such a committee was formed only in the U.K., where it has proved to be of considerable value. It is accountable to the group of Church Leaders and Coordinators of l'Arche in the U.K. and brings together representatives from each of the U.K. communities. The committee maintains contact with the ecumenical bodies of different churches and with members of the inter-church process "Not Strangers but Pilgrims," as well as with the Association of Interchurch Families (a network which offers support for inter-church and "mixed" marriages and provides a voice for such families in the churches). In response to the expressed needs of communities we have produced papers on "Healing a Wound"[18] (subsequently adopted for use by the European Commission on Ecumenism [1991-1993]) and "Blessing at the Time of Communion."

---

[18] *Ecumenism in l'Arche* (2).

North America Zone

The Commission on Ecumenism for Canada and the United States included among its members Father Tom Ryan, director of the Canadian Centre for Ecumenism, based in Montreal. In 1986 the Commission asked communities of l'Arche about their ecumenical experience and concerns. These were wide-ranging, but one which related particularly to their people with handicaps is especially poignant: "How do we explain to our handicapped members, who speak the language of the heart which makes all things simple, the theological subtleties and intellectual nuances that separate the Christian churches?"

The Commission tried to respond to these questions. Father Tom Ryan and Bishop Peter Sutton, at that time liaison bishop for l'Arche with the Pontifical Council for the Laity in Rome,[19] wrote to all communities indicating ways forward but more particularly affirming them in what they were living: "You already are where the churches-at-large are being called to go... All those working today in the field of ecumenism are saying with one voice that the agenda for the next decade is *sharing of life and faith* at local levels. . . What the churches need at the moment are those who are willing to live the suffering of our divisions. It is not easy to embrace the suffering of constantly having to confront and absorb our brokenness."

A year or two later Tom Ryan helped communities to see both the challenge and the opportunity within their ecumenical vocation by calling attention to what he described as three seminal notions:

1. "Host and guest," or "getting people into each other's rooms in the Christian household." Most people have no idea what the "ritual language with God" is *like* in another church.
2. "Voluntary displacement," which calls us to distance ourselves from the comfortable and secure. If we do this we experience our true condition as pilgrims on the way. Tom Ryan pointed out that there was within l'Arche an opportunity to realize this notion of "voluntary displacement" as well as that of "host and guest" when assistants of one tradition

---

19   Bishop Sutton had been asked to fulfil this role by the International Council and had agreed to "accompany" l'Arche in this way.

accompanied handicapped people to their own church of another tradition.

3. The biblical notion of *kenosis* or emptying, which implies conversion, sacrifice, and dying at both a personal and institutional level. In Chapter 2 of the Letter to the Philippians, St. Paul describes the essence of community life and takes us straight into the life of the Trinity as source and model of community. Here *kenosis* or emptying of self are the ultimate means at our disposal. It is a passage of scripture well known to many in l'Arche since it forms part of the liturgy of the washing of the feet in interdenominational covenant retreats, during which participants announce the covenant. (See page 23.)

So if there is any encouragement in Christ, any incentive of love, any participation in the Spirit, any affection and sympathy, complete my joy by being of the same mind, having the same love, being in full accord and of one mind. Do nothing from selfishness or conceit, but in humility count others better than yourselves. Let each of you look not only to his own interests, but also to the interests of others. Have this mind among yourselves, which was in Christ Jesus who, though he was in the form of God, did not count equality with God a thing to be grasped, but emptied himself, taking the form of a servant, being born in the likeness of men. And being found in human form he humbled himself and became obedient unto death, even death on a cross.

(Philippians 2:1-8)

It was particularly difficult for the North American Commission to propose ecumenical guidelines, the situation being much more complex here than, for example, in the U.K. North America presents such a wide diversity of Christian churches, embracing the historic "mainline" churches (Anglican, Lutheran, Orthodox, Presbyterian, Roman Catholic, United), together with a great number of American-born movements and evangelical churches, and this wide array is reflected in North American l'Arche communities.

Asia – West Pacific Zone

From the creation of Ecumenical Commissions in 1987, the Asia – West pacific Zone Council decided that the ecumenical needs of communities in Australia and India needed to be addressed separately despite the fact that they belonged to the same Zone. Eileen Glass was responsible for a Regional Ecumenical Commission in Australia and Hazel Bradley for a Commission in India. As Hazel was Zone Coordinator, she made every effort to attend the meetings of both Commissions.

Australia

As in Europe and North America, questions were raised concerning interdenominational retreats, relationships with local churches of different denominations, preparation of people with handicaps for membership of a church, accompanying people with handicaps to Sunday worship, and work with national and diocesan ecumenical committees.

The Commission also considered a paper written by Eileen Glass in 1989 on the spirituality of l'Arche in Australia. The history, culture and spirituality of Australia were examined alongside the spirituality of l'Arche. It was pointed out that much of community life in l'Arche is founded on the pain and suffering of people with mental handicaps and of their families. The aboriginal people, whose sense of belonging, of community and unity with the land was so vulnerable to the arrival of white people, have also known suffering, rejection and a sense of dislocation and violation of sacred relationships with the earth. Then there is the guilt attached to such treatment of aboriginal people by white people, and white Australians also carry memories of the deep suffering and pain of a people transported to that country, severed from family and place of belonging, rejected and condemned.

Much of the history of Australia results in a fierce individualism and deep-rooted suspicion of authority; there is also a quest for authenticity which is in part a search for healing. These are all aspects to be taken into account when working towards unity among Christians and in Australian society.[20]

---

[20]   Eileen Glass, *Some Reflections on the Spirituality of l'Arche in Australia*, Canberra, 1989.

Regular meetings of a Commission were difficult to organize because of distance and a shortage of assistants, but dialogue took place during the Regional Council and at other meetings. There was general recognition that for too long the vision and spirituality of l'Arche had been expressed largely in Western and Christian terms, with the result that some members of Asha Niketan who were Hindu or Muslim felt marginalized. One consequence was that inter-faith subjects were avoided for fear of hurting or dividing people. In 1992 a conscious decision was taken to tackle the inter-faith dimension of the Region in a practical and positive way: Hindus would agree to dispense with numerous images in community places of prayer, Muslims and Protestants would accept oil lamps and incense, Roman Catholics would become more open to different ways of praying. There has been agreement that three types of inter-faith retreats are needed in India: one based on nature and reflecting the profound sense of God in all creation, another on meditation (*Nama Japam* or repetition of the name of God) and finally a retreat based on the spirituality of life with the poor, the spirituality of l'Arche.

Vision and reality

During the period in which the ecumenical commissions were meeting (1987-1993) considerable energy was also going into the founding and support of new communities as well as the revision of structures. Many communities were also experiencing serious difficulties: there was a shortage of assistants, particularly those able and willing to live in community households for more than a year or two; government funding was becoming dependent on increasingly complex regulations and interdenominational and inter-faith communities were finding it particularly difficult to focus and articulate their vision within specific situations.

At all levels within the Federation there was uncertainty as to how best to make daily life more viable for assistants, especially those living in community households. (A number had always lived elsewhere, for example, in their own apartments, while working within the community.) Significant progress began to be made in 1995 when a full session of the International Spirituality Commission (which brings together the chairperson of commissions on Ecumenism, Celibacy, Covenant and Families, throughout the world and the International Council) was devoted to The Vocation of Assistants.

There is no doubt that the commissions were contributing to the widening gap between the vision and development of l'Arche on the one hand, and the reality of daily life within communities on the other. The communities, for example, had pressing priorities which were unrelated to ecumenism and the last thing they needed were papers upon which to reflect or guidelines which many found irritating.

The situation in 1995

The mandates of all commissions were abruptly terminated in 1993 because the International Council considered that each of the Zones, which had now increased from three to seven, should take responsibility for setting up its own commissions – ecumenical and other – in order to concentrate on matters most relevant to its own needs.

This was part of an ongoing policy of decentralisation in the Federation, but did not take full account of the shortage of long-term assistants with the necessary experience and available time to participate in commissions.

As a consequence, there are at present only two Commissions on Ecumenism within l'Arche. One of these is in the South Europe Zone where the great majority of communities are Roman Catholic, although there is an interdenominational community of long standing in Switzerland and a more recent foundation in Hungary. The second Commission is in North America. In fact, it is a co-operative work of two Zones: Eastern and Western North America.

For the three Zones of North Europe, Latin America – Caribbean, and Africa, and for the two Regions of India and Australia within the Asia – West Pacific Zone, there are Spirituality Commissions. These are made up of four to six people who, between them, cover ecumenism, celibacy, covenant and family. In the past *each* of these aspects would have been matter for a separate commission.

The ecumenical commission of the South Europe Zone is extremely important, in that it ensures that their twenty to twenty-five Roman Catholic communities give a certain priority to the ecumenical vocation of the Zone. Equally, the new communities in eastern Europe and projects in the Middle East raise the important matter of relationships with Orthodox churches. In North America, ecumenical awareness and sensitivity are needed because of the diversity of "belonging" in the American and Canadian communities. The whole of l'Arche will benefit from the input and experience of these two Zones, where ecumenical reflection is a priority.

4

Belonging to our parishes

I like to go to church for the readings and singing hymns, to belong to Jesus, to meet friends. I go to St. John's because I'm in l'Arche and I'm an Anglican. There are lots of children. It's lively and fun. John, the vicar, takes the service – we say prayers, sing hymns and have communion.

Barbara Fraughan, L'Arche Liverpool

Belonging to a parish is enormously important for many people with mental handicaps. Barbara is probably right in saying that she "goes to St. John's because I'm in l'Arche and I'm an Anglican." Even within the context of a l'Arche community there can be difficulty in attending a parish church. People with mental handicaps are not always easily accepted in parish congregations: some may need assistance in getting to church, and others may need help in communication and in enabling people in the parish to understand their behaviour. Initially, a link needs to be made with the local church and appropriate information provided about l'Arche and its ecumenical stance.

In most l'Arche communities members attend their local parish or parishes and it is very exceptional for a community to have its own Sunday services. The first community in Trosly is one such exception, which came about because there was no church in the village in 1964 when the community began. People from the village now participate in services in the large community chapel, which has in fact become the local parish church.

For interdenominational communities Sunday morning can feel more like a marathon than the day of the Lord! It would not be unusual for eight or nine members of a single community household to go to three or four different parishes.

In the U.K. it is not uncommon for a community to relate to as many as eight different parishes. The principal connections are with Anglican and Roman Catholic parishes (reflecting our denominational "belonging"), but the U.K. communities are also involved with Methodist, Baptist, United Reformed Church and Presbyterian congregations. Assistants are often asked to accompany people with mental handicaps to *their* church whose tradition and liturgy may well be unfamiliar to the assistant. The assistants may need an opportunity to discuss their reactions to this and discover meaning in what they are doing. They may also find in it the opportunity for that *voluntary displacement* of which Tom Ryan speaks (see pages 41 and 59).

At an inter-faith level, Vishwanathan in the Kerala community in India, a Hindu and mentally handicapped, was happy to go to church at Christmas and so taught Christian assistants that they too should be more open to other Faiths. Speaking of the Asha Niketan community, he would say: "In this place, plenty of place [space], we should make a temple for prayer here for everybody. Why do we go to all these different places?" As Maggie Smith writes:

> By choosing to be with people with mental handicaps, assistants have been led into doing something ecumenical. There is something very real in this: being alongside the person who is poor and weak inevitably draws one to the places where God wants reconciliation and makes one both a receiver and an agent of reconciliation. Presence at the "other" church is in itself a statement of thirst for unity, respect for the tradition of the "other" and a means of valuing it; all this is immensely important for the person with a mental handicap who belongs to that church.[21]

---

[21]   *Guidelines for Working with Local Parishes.*

48

Our vision of ourselves may not correspond to the image we present to parish clergy and fellow parishioners: while groups from l'Arche can be disturbing and disruptive, this is certainly not always the case. Furthermore, given time, good communication and goodwill on both sides, our presence is frequently life-giving and comes to be valued by the other members of the parishes to which we belong.

It is important to provide parish clergy gradually and systematically with information about l'Arche,[22] and this should include details of our ecumenical stance and of the different ways in which the community has chosen to live the reality of its inter-church existence. Sometimes parish clergy are invited to celebrate the eucharist within the community; they will need to be aware of the struggle in the community to hold together both loyalty to our churches' conflicting disciplines over intercommunion and respect for individual conscience. For instance, in the U.K. communities there are generally agreed-upon and understood reasons for acting in solidarity with the different local churches to which we belong and we are concerned not to move faster than is possible for our different denominations.

Parish clergy will also need to know the importance of the blessing given to those not receiving communion and of the need for touch within this context. It is also important that those who administer the elements of communion during parish services are aware of the need to bless people who request this in a church to which they do not belong.[23]

Members of the clergy, and particularly those who are single or celibate, can find l'Arche households especially welcoming. Many interdenominational communities invite clergy from local parishes to regular meetings, as well as to meals and other community events, and the community leader of l'Arche Lambeth and a small number of assistants from that community meet the Anglican, Baptists, Methodist and Roman Catholic ministers three times a year. Our agenda over the past two years has included:

---

22   *Guidelines for Working with Local Parishes.*
23   *Blessing at the Time of Communion.*

49

- The spirituality of people with mental handicaps
- The ecumenical dimension of l'Arche
- The vocation of assistants in l'Arche
- The contemplative dimension in l'Arche (vocation of assistants and people with mental handicaps)
- A day in the life of a community household.

With the help of church leaders of different traditions who accompany l'Arche in the U.K., it has also been possible to arrange for gatherings of local clergy of different denominations for a few days of retreat and dialogue with long-term assistants.

The Week of Prayer for Christian Unity can provide a particular opportunity for communities to relate to their parishes and a number of communities contribute to the special interdenominational "joint services" of that week. In 1996 the Lambeth community performed a simple, silent mime in the middle of such a service: two people wearing silver paper crowns represented Power and Riches and stood near the altar, while others walked slowly around the congregation: two represented homeless and hungry people who were begging, two were "disabled" and another took the part of an elderly woman walking painfully. Their slow silent walk said everything. Another opportunity to relate to parishes arises when we organize a week-long Ignatian "guided retreat in daily life" within the community, and invite local people of different traditions to participate.

Men and women with mental handicaps frequently come to l'Arche without any experience of "church" and it takes time to discover their "story" and that of their family: whether or not they have been baptized and whether any Faith background exists. It is then a question of whether or not they wish to be involved in any church "belonging," and, if so, to which denomination. This process requires long and careful discernment involving all concerned. Preparing people to receive the sacraments and for full membership of the particular church can also be an opportunity to work across the usual denominational boundaries. In the mid-1980s the Lambeth community obtained the consent of local Anglican and Roman Catholic parish clergy to prepare four mentally handicapped members of the community together: one for confirmation in the Anglican Church, another for baptism and confirmation in the same church; one for communion in the Roman Catholic Church and the fourth for baptism, communion and confirmation in the Roman Catholic Church. This preparation was carried out over two years within the context of a specially constituted "Faith Group", and on a particular spring Sunday the whole community accompanied the four women to two separate parish services in which each of the four became a full member of her church.

Assistants and the four women concerned subsequently expressed the wish that the "Faith Group" should continue and there are now a number of Faith Groups in the Lambeth community. Each one consists of six or eight people meeting in pairs – an assistant and a man or woman with a handicap, who come together for a couple of hours twice a month in order to focus on some aspect of scripture or the Christian year, usually taking a particular theme for a particular year. The meeting of the Faith Group is a time of prayer and sharing through words, music, song, mime, drawing, or just being together, and similar groups exist in many l'Arche communities in the U.K. and elsewhere under a variety of names.

A few years ago Maggie Smith and Vincent Dunkling of the Kent community worked together in order to enable Vincent to discern the church to which he wished to belong. When Vincent came to l'Arche in 1975 he was a member of the Church of England and chose to attend the eucharist each week at the nearby university chaplaincy. He became a valued member of the Anglican community there and with their support chose to be confirmed, which meant a lot to him. Vincent is very sociable and fairly independent, and he also decided to go regularly to a prayer group at the local Roman Catholic church. He would periodically express the wish to become a Roman Catholic. At the same time he was finding that being part of a changing population of students at the university chaplaincy was becoming less attractive and that he wished to join a local city parish in order to experience an Anglican Church community more fully. However, as it was clear that the question of becoming a Roman Catholic was also serious, Maggie Smith undertook a process of discernment with him which lasted eighteen months, during which Vincent and Maggie met regularly and, on several occasions, Vincent alone met with the minister of his Anglican parish and also with the parish priest of the Roman Catholic church. Vincent is able to read and a summary of every conversation and details of any decision were written by those in dialogue with Vincent, in a special book which he kept so that the record of what had taken place was available for him and for those he was consulting.

For Vincent – as for anyone making such a decision – it was important to discern the deepest God-given desire of his heart. Because of his mental handicap, it was essential to provide effective support in order to help him to make his decision.

A final decision to ask for reception into the Catholic Church was reached after a short personal "retreat" which Vincent made with the help of Maggie, the minister of his Anglican parish and a Roman Catholic priest who is a friend of long standing. He enrolled in the RCIA programme[24] in the local Roman Catholic parish and followed this faithfully over several months. The following Easter Vincent was received into the Roman Catholic Church with his companions in the RCIA group. The entire process from Vincent's first expression of a serious wish to join the Roman Catholic Church up to his reception into that church took two-and-a-half years.

Community Pastoral Ministers and local parishes

For many years the International Council of l'Arche has encouraged communities to appoint pastoral ministers with a particular concern for the Christian vision and spiritual life of the community. The task of the pastoral minister is to work closely with the community leader who needs support in the pastoral and spiritual aspects of leadership. Obviously community leaders have a pastoral duty to care for and nourish the members of the community and are not called simply to be good administrators. However, if the same person is asked to exercise a managerial-leadership role *and* a pastoral-spiritual role, the person concerned can find themselves unable to exercise either role adequately, because the managerial aspect relates primarily to justice and the pastoral-spiritual role to compassion.

In the case of Roman Catholic communities, the local bishop is asked to nominate a priest, a member of a religious order, or a

---

[24]   Rite of Christian Initiation of Adults.

lay person to fulfil the pastoral-spiritual role. This is very seldom a full-time appointment.

The process is more complex for interdenominational communities and is established in consultation with the church leaders of different Christian traditions who accompany l'Arche in a particular country. It is likely that parish clergy of different traditions are already involved with the community, either because they celebrate community eucharists or exercise pastoral care of members of l'Arche who belong to their parish. Local clergy must therefore be consulted when the community is considering the appointment of a pastoral minister, as one of the main responsibilities of the person concerned is to work closely with local parishes in order to enable people with mental handicaps who so wish to take a full part in the life of their local churches, and to transmit the spirituality and ecumenical dimension of l'Arche to the leaders of local churches.

5

The eucharist

The Last Supper

A careful reading of the Gospels is a salutary reminder that
the last meal that Jesus shared with his close friends was hardly
a moment of unity and harmony. "With desire I have desired to
eat this passover with you. . . " (Luke 22:15, King James). Taken
together, the four accounts of that evening provide evidence of
pettiness, incomprehension, ambition, division and treachery. In
the middle of all this Jesus asks to be remembered in thanksgiving, in the blessing and breaking of bread and in sharing the
cup of wine – the eucharist.

Unlike Matthew, Mark and Luke, John makes no mention of
this. His memory is of Jesus washing his feet and washing the
feet of the others.

In the midst of the messiness and meanness of humanity, at
this particular moment, this last meal with his closest friends and
followers, and in his near despair, the only thing that Jesus feels
able to do is to get down on his knees and wash their feet. Then
he tells them that they will be blessed if they will do the same
for each other. And having shown them by washing their feet the
kind of love he means, he passionately exhorts them to love one
another as he has loved them.

At the Last Supper Jesus charges his friends to *do* two things:
"*Do* this in remembrance of me" – the eucharist – and, "If I then,
your Lord and Teacher, have washed your feet, you also ought to

wash one another's feet. For I have given you an example, that you also should "*do* as I have done to you" (John 13:14-15).

We who are many . . .

In so many of our l'Arche communities we find ourselves divided at the eucharist because we belong to different Christian traditions. But we know that the deepest bonds between us lie in our vulnerable common humanity. That humanity, with all its weakness and pain, its divisions, faults and failings, is reflected in the divisions at the eucharist. There our present reality is acknowledged, suffered and blessed as opening onto another future.

The sacrament in which we can *fully* share, in which we can fully participate, is the washing of the feet. This we only celebrate in a literal "liturgical" form once or twice a year, but the significance of washing one another's feet is celebrated daily in the realities and messiness of community life, a life which contains all of the components of division and disharmony that were present at the Last Supper, and more.

As Christians who are trying to heal their own divisions as they enter into dialogue with other Faiths, one of the most frequent questions we face concerns the meaning of scriptural passages which affirm that the only way to God is through Jesus and his cross; for example, John 14:6: "I am the way, the truth and the life; no one comes to the Father, but by me." Surely the way to God must necessarily pass through God's own incarnation: his total identification with vulnerable and suffering humanity. "I was hungry and you gave me food, I was thirsty and you gave me drink... was a stranger... in prison...." This passage on the last judgement in Matthew 25 surely means that the way to God is through suffering humanity. In Christian terms it is there that Jesus is to be found.

The rigid barriers which used to exist between Christians of differing traditions and between different World Faiths are diminishing, despite lingering antagonisms. One of the consequences of the breaking down of barriers has been that people of very different religious backgrounds as well as those who acknowledge no specific religious affiliation are working closely together in many fields having to do with the relief of suffering.

56

These areas include the hospice movement for the care of those who are dying, assistance for people with AIDS as well as for men, women and children suffering from drug abuse, and initiatives for the homeless, for refugees and for prisoners. And then there are those like ourselves who live and work alongside people with mental handicaps. All who are involved in such work live close to their hearts and, in Christian terms, close to the cross.

Our society generally considers that people so obviously in need of help have nothing to give and everything to gain in any caring relationship. Those who do the caring know otherwise and frequently speak out. I believe that it is in these places of encounter between those who are perceived as "care-givers" and "cared for" that ecumenism is experienced most deeply and fruitfully and that all those involved are being called to unity. Many who live close to their hearts carry within themselves a sense of fragmentation, loss and lack of recognition. One could include here so many young people who feel lost in the face of the dismemberment of values in our society.

All these people, and others besides, call urgently for unity within themselves and within those who surround them. They call for unity within the fragmented Christian church and for a healing of the rift which exists within the religious dimension of humanity. In *The Testing of Hearts*, based on a personal journal he kept while Rector of the Ecumenical Institute at Tantur near Jerusalem, Donald Nicholl reflects on the ceremony of eating unleavened bread during the Week of Prayer for Christian Unity.[25]

> We are soon to eat matza, i.e., unleavened bread, the bread of affliction as it is termed in the Scripture.... May I suggest to you that we should think of what we are about to do as a token of our determination, each in our own calling, truly to eat the bread of affliction by sharing our energies, our very lives, with those who alone give meaning to our ceremony? Those who in the literal sense of the word eat matza, the bread of affliction. Those in prison.... the homeless.... the hungry, the sick and the lonely...,

---

[25] Page 145.

By eating the bread of affliction together we have signified in God's presence our determination to work for the day when no one whosoever will be hungry or in prison or homeless or lonely or sick. Perhaps that is precisely the manner in which we are called to work in the present age so that under God's providence even Christian unity will be achieved. First the bread of affliction; and only then the bread of the Eucharist.

Division at the eucharist originates in and reflects the divisions, faults and failings of human beings: the divisions within ourselves, our communities, our societies, between weak and strong, rich and poor, hungry and replete....

Sharing each meal in the community households of l'Arche is a sign of sharing the bread of affliction, sharing the lives of people with mental handicaps. Some twelve years ago, an incident which was initiated in the Lambeth community by a man with Down's syndrome who has since died showed us the connection between sharing the bread of affliction and the possibility that one day, through this, we might share the bread of the eucharist. Nick was distressed by the fact that we separate on Sundays to go to different churches. As a devout Anglican he participated in the eucharist each Sunday. He also came regularly to community eucharists where he experienced division. One evening after supper he brought bread and water to the table where he had eaten with his companions, blessed the bread and the water, gave them to his friends, took some himself, gave thanks, and said, "Now we have all been to communion together."

Our Christian churches will only eat of the bread of eucharist together when all have learned to eat the bread of affliction; they will only drink of the same cup when all have learned to drink from the cup of suffering of those who are poor and oppressed.

No Christian community can be built up unless it has its basis and centre in the celebration of the most Holy Eucharist. Here, therefore, all education in the spirit of community must originate. If this celebration is to be sincere and thorough, it must lead to various works of charity and mutual help, as well as to missionary activity and to different forms of Christian witness.

I vividly remember reading this passage from *The Decree on the Ministry and Life of Priests* in the documents of Vatican II (Ch. 2, I, 6) in 1974, shortly after we had made the painful decision not to participate fully in the eucharist of one another's churches in the first U.K. l'Arche community near Canterbury. I wondered angrily where this document left us, since the eucharist could not be the basis and centre of our lives as a Christian community. Others in the community were also disappointed, angry, sad and confused. Inevitably we projected difficulties in our personal relationships onto the decision that we should abide by the rules of the Roman Catholic Church regarding the eucharist, a decision with which not everyone agreed.

Anything to do with the eucharist touches the heart – and the gut! – and perhaps this is particularly so in l'Arche, where assistants have to learn to exist alongside people who live at the level of the heart and express what they feel at gut level. We too are obviously vulnerable to feelings which stem from our own deep-seated needs and personal experience of pain.

Christians seeking to take some of the necessary steps towards unity need to experience what Tom Ryan describes as *voluntary displacement:* a moving away from the comfortable and secure, from what we know and take for granted. This process, of course, involves a sense of loss as well as an intellectual understanding, a sense of history and the acceptance of differences in church doctrine. Tom Ryan emphasizes that a *kenosis* or self-emptying is involved, a letting-go, a dying which inevitably involves some suffering or pain.

Eucharist in the community

From the beginning there have been three characteristics of a l'Arche community: the central place of people with mental handicaps, the value of eucharistic worship and an openness to those of any Faith or none. Like many of God's gifts these essential characteristics have not been easy to handle. The early Roman Catholic communities in France soon became aware that the few Protestants among them felt excluded and marginalized when they found that, as members of other Christian churches, they could not normally be invited to receive communion at a Roman Catholic eucharist. Eucharistic hospitality was slow to develop, and even when it was offered, it was sometimes experienced by members of other churches as a reluctant concession.

In North America and in the U.K. we became aware that community celebration of the eucharist was a potential minefield. Communities quickly found themselves faced with regulations regarding the reception of communion, and realized that the rules of their different churches were irreconcilable. The principal difference lay in the canon law of the Roman Catholic Church, which does not normally allow members of other denominations to receive communion at its eucharist, nor does it permit its own members to receive communion at the eucharist of other churches. Particular rules apply vis-à-vis the question of intercommunion between members of the Roman Catholic Church and the Orthodox Churches. The rules are irreconcilable, however, as Roman Catholics are in fact permitted by their own church to receive communion at an Orthodox eucharist if they are unable to attend a Roman Catholic one, while the Orthodox Churches will not normally permit Roman Catholics to receive communion under any circumstances, nor will they allow their own members to receive communion at a Roman Catholic eucharist. In a similar way the Anglican communion welcomes baptized communicant members of other denominations to the eucharist, but Roman Catholics are not normally permitted to accept the invitation.

All churches, of course, have rules regarding the reception of the eucharist and in 1954 the World Alliance of Reformed Churches (which brings together churches with a Presbyterian polity) formulated a policy of "the open table" in the Princeton Declaration, since "the table is the Lord's, not ours" – although not all Reformed churches adhered to the policy. In 1972 the Church of England first issued the general invitation to baptized communicant members of other churches which hold the doctrine of the Trinity. It is also the case that all churches have certain expectations of communicant members, even if these are not defined as "rules": for instance, confirmation would become an issue in the Anglican Church if a Roman Catholic, deciding to ignore the rules of their own church, regularly received communion at that eucharist. Churches of the Reformation would justifiably want to be consulted if, for whatever reason, their members were regularly receiving communion at a Roman Catholic eucharist, as a result of some dispensation from the Roman Catholic side.

The pain experienced by many Roman Catholics in interdenominational communities could be expressed in the words: "The eucharist is at the heart of my relationship with Jesus, at the heart of my church, and it is indescribably painful to witness this sacrament of unity becoming a source of division." The invitation voiced at a Reformed church eucharist is equally painful if one is not at liberty to respond: "The table is the Lord's, not ours. It is made ready for those who love him and want to love him more." Those who do not receive appear to refuse the invitation.

In many Roman Catholic l'Arche communities permission has been given for eucharistic hospitality to be offered to individual Protestant or Anglican members under the usual conditions required by the Roman Catholic Church:

- danger of death and other pressing need;
- inability to approach a minister of their own church;
- a spontaneous request to receive the sacrament which may be granted on condition that the person manifest Catholic faith in this sacrament and be properly disposed.

If, however, assistants visit or move to an interdenominational community, they are likely to find themselves in a somewhat different situation. In the U.K., for example, Anglican and Protestant assistants can receive communion at eucharists celebrated by either of these churches, at which Roman Catholics can receive a blessing; conversely, Anglicans and Protestants would be offered a blessing rather than communion at a community Roman Catholic eucharist. In both cases they experience division.

It is not uncommon for members of Protestant or Reformed churches to express a sense of exclusion in other ways: "Celebration of the eucharist in my church is not central to our worship. The fact that it has such an important place in your worship and in your discussions about ecumenical matters makes me feel even more excluded than when I am not offered communion."

In most communities there are a few people who experience matters in yet another way: "The rules and regulations of the churches have nothing to do with the message of Jesus. I'm a Christian, I want to follow Jesus. I don't want to belong to any particular church. Churches tend to divide."

In the U.K. some assistants who have experienced these divisions for ten or even twenty years are now asking: "How long do we have to go on like this? After twenty years of not receiving communion at the eucharist of another church, not only has there been no shift in the position of the churches, but I do not believe that there is any understanding on the part of the churches of the pain and frustration in communities like ours."

And what do our people with mental handicaps feel? For many of them it has been a new experience to make contact with and be accepted by any church. It has sometimes been a question of discovering whether or not they have been baptized into a church and, if so, whether they wished to pursue the commitment thus made on their behalf. This has involved them in making a choice, which requires time and preparation, and it has frequently become very important for them to belong to their parish church and to participate in services as full members. The same importance is attached to the reception of communion within eucharistic services in their own community. So what do they feel when offered a blessing rather than communion at eucharistic services of other traditions?

Their reactions are as varied as those of assistants, though for some their experience of loss and exclusion throughout their lives leads them to expect this and live with it. After ten years in the Lambeth community, Philip is able to say, "At first I felt very sad when I could not go to communion [at a Roman Catholic eucharist], but now not so much. When I receive communion the Spirit of God comes into my heart. I feel it here in my body (placing his hand over his heart). When I receive a blessing I feel very holy (moving his hand downward from his head). I feel comforted and then I comfort people who are not so well."

Robert, in the Liverpool community, is less verbal than Philip. An assistant describes an episode: "Robert always seems very keen to come to community eucharists. He obviously likes them, but he has little time for debate on intercommunion.

When Fr. John tried to give him a blessing, Robert said: "Stop messing around, John!"

On another occasion Robert elicited an important reflection from an Archbishop of Canterbury while he was celebrating the eucharist in an interdenominational congregation. Dr. Robert Runcie tells the story in his foreword to my book *Nick: Man of the Heart:*

> There was a man called Robert. We shared the same name and the same birth place in Liverpool. A casual observer might have dismissed him as awkward and inarticulate. He presented himself in a line with those coming up for communion or a blessing. Robert seemed uncertain what he was asking for. Finally, he took the host, looked at it and then broke it in two and handed half of it back to me. There could have been no better expression of the truth that we are spiritually nourished not by the owning but the sharing of Christ's gift.

My memory of that episode is that when Dr. Runcie, visibly moved, passed near Robert at the end of the eucharist, the latter grasped him firmly by the hand and walked the rest of the way down the aisle with the Archbishop. Few if any of us are likely to extend a hand to an Archbishop who is visibly moved, whether in compassion, solidarity or friendship. Maybe we need to ask ourselves why... but for Robert from Liverpool who had broken the host and given half back to the Archbishop, it was no problem. For the Archbishop I hope it was a gift.

In the Kent community an assistant describes a Roman Catholic eucharist in which Anne[26] approached the priest and was reminded by signs from an assistant to fold her arms in order to receive a blessing. She stood still for the blessing and then, on walking away, turned, stuck out her tongue at the priest and the host, and swore.

Taken in isolation, that account might elicit questions such as, "How appropriate is it for Anne to be allowed to be at the service at all, and/or to come for a blessing?" or, "Why do you

---

[26]   This is not her real name.

impose these incomprehensible rules on people with mental handicaps? Why not follow their simplicity and directness? They are leading us in their own need for unity; why not follow them?" This latter point is frequently voiced in rather more theological terms by those who know and value our communities but do not understand our position vis-à-vis the institutional churches. (See Chapter 4.)

In the case of Anne, however, a greater understanding is needed of *who she is*. The assistant describing the incident continues: "Anne is a woman in her early forties who has lived in this community for ten years. She knows how to celebrate and enjoy herself, and community life and harmonious relationships are important to her. Having a certain amount of interior disturbance, Anne relies a lot on outward unity to help her feel that everything is OK in the world. I have come to these conclusions by observing Anne, as she has very little language and is therefore unable to describe her experiences. Since coming to the community, prayers and church have become very important to her. On holiday, when out of routine, the rest of us may forget about prayers at the end of the day, but not Anne." In the light of her knowledge of Anne the assistant interprets what took place at the eucharist as follows: "I noticed Anne looking happy and expectant as she wound her way through the chairs to the priest. The assistant with her had reminded her that she would not receive communion. She had obviously not understood, or chosen to ignore, both the earlier explanation and the more immediate one. Now the truth was apparent. She was here at this service, she had understood an invitation by Jesus, by the priest, by the people around her, and yet she was to be refused. I imagine she felt cheated, deprived and possibly rejected."

Anne had certainly been at many community eucharists and would have received a blessing on many occasions. What was it that triggered her anger and distress this time? Those caring for her would certainly have tried to determine the cause and would seek to avoid a similar situation in the future. It is particularly important to do this if such episodes occur repeatedly and it is important to talk things over with the presiding minister, in order to decide what to do for the best. But there are no easy solutions!

64

The eucharist in larger gatherings

During international retreats and other gatherings, tension around the celebration of the eucharist becomes even more complex. The majority of participants at the event arrive with their personal, community, national and church experience of attempting to live ecumenically within diverse settings. Roman Catholics from communities in France or Belgium can find it inconceivable not to receive daily communion at a Roman Catholic eucharist, as they do in their own communities. This presents difficulties, because the daily eucharist at such gatherings is nearly always celebrated in different traditions: usually Anglican, Roman Catholic and Reformed or Lutheran. Those coming from Germany, for instance, may find it inconceivable *not* to receive communion at the eucharist regardless of which denomination is celebrating. Others from North America may feel that the eucharist should not be celebrated at all unless communion is offered to everyone. Representatives from U.K. communities are familiar with the experience of attending eucharists of different denominations while obeying the rules regarding the reception of communion, and will expect to be blessed when they do not receive. Some do not agree with this policy and as individuals will, in conscience, go beyond the rules.

Much of the above will be familiar to those who live or work in other interdenominational communities or who lead retreats or other gatherings which bring together Christians of different denominations. I well understand the remark of Donald Nicholl in *The Testing of Hearts:* "Every time I think we have exhausted the list of variations that can be played upon the theme of eucharistic dispute, someone comes up with yet another."

And yet by facing and acknowledging such problems and much pain, we have found ways of celebrating the eucharist together in interdenominational retreats and at international gatherings. While they are provisional and imperfect, they have still been real means of grace and moments of blessing and peace for those who have shared in them.

The meaning and transformation of pain

What is the pain, distress and near despair which so many feel when experiencing division at the eucharist? For some it is the pain of the dreadful reality of our broken body, the Church: the scandal of division and separation at the sacrament of unity in which we remember the risen Jesus whose body was broken for humankind and the whole of creation. This can resonate with the pain of separation which we all experience and carry within us at so many levels, particularly those with mental handicaps, whose lives have been fraught with separation. This is certainly the case for Anne. The pain may also relate to difficult and broken relationships within the community, which are projected onto eucharistic divisions.

The suffering can become so intolerable that individuals and communities seek at all costs to lessen the pain: perhaps by ceasing to celebrate the eucharist within the community so that individuals simply attend their own parish churches. Alternatively, wider eucharistic hospitality may be sought, at which point intercommunion probably becomes the aim with interdenominational communities, since these are unlikely to opt for "unity" at the Roman Catholic eucharist. Such "unity" would result if eucharistic hospitality were offered by special permission of the local Roman Catholic bishop and with the agreement of other local churches, because of the special circumstances of a l'Arche community.

Frequently, however, the pain is denied, questions are not raised and feelings are left unresolved within a community. Yet pain is a danger signal, ignored by the body or the psyche at serious cost. Our churches are a body with an inheritance of woundedness and rejection, as well as mutual hostility, ignorance and suspicion. But at last there is a sincere desire, within our churches, to understand and love one another and, where possible, to find agreement.

It is, I believe, this very opportunity for reconciliation which is at stake if we ignore the pain of separation at the eucharist. In the same way that we fail to integrate personal griefs and losses into our lives until we experience them in our hearts, our *feelings*, so we shall not integrate our past history of bitter division and woundedness between the Christian churches unless we *feel* the pain of it, and thus find the energy and motivation to transform pain into new life.

Division at the eucharist originates in the divisions, faults and failings of human beings. In a similar way the misery, injustice and pain of our world is reflected in the separation we experience at the eucharist. Stephen Verney[27] helped us to see some meaning in the pain and a way in which it can be transformed:

> When Jesus said, "Do this in remembrance of me" he was saying more than "Celebrate the eucharist," though he was saying that too. He was asking his friends to do as he did, live as he lived, love as he loved, give of themselves as he gave.... You *are* eucharistic communities: take the bread, receive the bread, which each of you is for the other, give thanks and bless, and experiencing the brokenness within you – give this bread that you are to each other.

Our communities are encouraged to think and talk about their experience of division at the eucharist, and to try to understand the reasons for this, and it is important that we regularly review our current policy regarding reception of communion, paying careful attention to the implications of any proposed changes.

Over the years we have learnt to understand and respect one another's positions, even when we disagree with them. We have also learnt to be increasingly gentle and caring in our relationships with each other and have discovered that, while rules and guidelines need to be respected and understood, they are not absolute and can sometimes be transcended by deeper principles of love and mercy.

We are one body

The need to be *together* at the eucharist is intimately linked to the broken and resurrected body of Jesus. It is also linked to a deep awareness of human brokenness associated with the body, the needs of the *person* as experienced in the body. When men and women have been deprived of gentle touch and tenderness in childhood or have been abused or ill-treated, they carry the

---

[27] Bishop Stephen Verney was one of the first Anglican bishops to accompany l'Arche in the U.K. (see page 36).

memory of that experience in the whole of their being, either consciously or unconsciously. Within l'Arche many people with mental handicaps carry a heavy burden of memory locked within their bodies. Some assistants carry similar memories, although active minds and keen intellects can obscure the pain, at least for a time. Respectful, gentle, tender care of bodies and a well-formed understanding of the needs of every person in this respect are an essential part of life in l'Arche.

This daily experience and attitude is consecrated each year on Maundy Thursday when we wash one another's feet, slowly, tenderly and reverently, and then anoint them with oil. In the same way the healing nature of gentle touch is highlighted in the giving of a blessing during community eucharists:

> One of the graces of communion is that it is physical: we eat, we drink. Blessing also needs to be communicated in a physical way. . .
>
> The reason for touch lies partly in the healing nature of blessing: Jesus often lightly touched those who were brought to him for healing. Blessing contains an action of God that is ultimately a mysterious gift. In developing a sense of this mystery there is a need to go beyond conceptual thought to physical action and symbol. Blessing is not wholly perceived conceptually, but needs perception at the level of the heart. In l'Arche this is particularly important as people with mental handicaps perceive more readily, or may only perceive at the level of the heart.[28]

---

[28]   *Blessing at the Time of Communion.*

6

The heart
of the matter

It has been said that ninety-five percent of ecumenism consists in developing friendship and trust between people. The word ecumenism comes from the Greek *oikos*, meaning "house," and *menein* – "to dwell" or "to remain." In Chapter 15, verse 9 of his Gospel, John uses the Greek word *menei*, "abide (dwell, rest in) my love," and in this discourse Jesus speaks of communion in the sense of the very deep relationship for which every human heart longs.

L'Arche began by "dwelling in a house" with people who have mental handicaps – trying to create community *with* them, and thus it has continued; the "house" has extended into workshops, farms, horticultural projects, as well as the homes of friends and into parishes and other places of worship. But as well as being a concrete reality, l'Arche is an *attitude* which can take root anywhere.

The vision of l'Arche and its ecumenical vocation have always been rooted in the immediate and pressing needs of people with mental handicaps, and our struggles to create community have always been rooted in the need to respond to and wrestle with the needs of those who live at the level of the heart. Their needs have to do with relationship in its deepest form: communion. In order to understand the ecumenical vocation of l'Arche, it is necessary to look more closely at what is actually involved in our community life. Although life at the level of the heart has to do

Jesus speaks of communion in the sense of the very deep relationship
for which every human heart longs

with feelings and emotions, there is a greater and deeper reality involved, which has to do with the fullness of being a person and the deepest needs of the human being.

Each one of us needs relationships based on faithfulness and truth. Père Thomas Philippe, Roman Catholic priest , theologian, philosopher, and co-founder of l'Arche, frequently reminded us that a person is an individual in relationship. He would speak of the heart as that place where the person exists and develops within relationships of love.

But the heart is not necessarily a comfortable place in which to live, particularly if that heart has been deprived of its most fundamental requirement: to love and be loved, and to belong and be valued for who one is. People with mental handicaps live very much at the level of the heart rather than the intellect, as do young children and very many people who, for whatever reason, frequently illness, deprivation and/or old age, discover that the heart takes precedence over the mind. Such people have little inclination or ability to live other than at the level of the heart, and men and women with mental handicaps are especially vulnerable to "heart-suffering," particularly if they are severely disabled.

Fruitful dialogue between Christians and between those of different Faiths depends largely on friendship and trust, and therefore on the quality of relationships between people. Our experience in l'Arche tells us that positive relationships are the most important requirement for powerless and vulnerable people if they are to live, grow and bear fruit. In trying to overcome the difficulties involved in creating such relationships we discover, of course, that the needs of every person are the same. The source and expression of our ecumenical vocation lie in our experience of building positive relationships, with all the joy and pain that this implies. This is the fundamental reality that l'Arche can share with the Christian churches and with those belonging to other Faiths, as they seek to establish greater mutual understanding. But we need to be clear about the implications of making the *quality* of relationships our principal focus and there is considerable complexity in creating relationships with mentally handicapped people.

The gifts and secondary handicaps
of people with mental handicaps

Many men and women with mental handicaps have gifts that warm the hearts of others: a capacity to welcome and accept people regardless of who they are or what they do; an intuitive understanding of the feelings of others; compassion; and an ability to live in the present and to rejoice with the glad and weep with the distressed. They have a capacity for wonder, for accepting the mystery which is at the heart of religious faith as well as the mysteries and wonders of nature and the universe. The ability to "accept" mystery is a sure way of finding meaning to life. Only by the acceptance of mystery can one possibly reconcile faith in a loving God with, say, the death of a child or young person. It is a matter of accepting something which is a scandal and needs to be recognized as such, while trusting that somehow, at some time, the meaning of this mystery will be revealed. Those who have been able to integrate experiences of loss into their lives alongside their experience of dependence have acquired a certain wisdom and peace. They have acquired an exceptional ability to trust and to relate to God and to others.

But the reality of the lives of people with mental handicaps is that negative experiences frequently result in "secondary handicaps" which are by far the more serious disability, however profound the primary disability of mental handicap. Experience tells them that they are a disappointment to their parents and their families, that they are "different" in a way that they frequently understand as "bad," because they are unable to do things that are simple for others and unable to understand what is being said and done around them. For some there is a deep sense of rejection, of being unloved and unlovable, of being evil. This of course leads to a variety of reactions: depression, anxiety, profound insecurity, withdrawal and loss of contact with external reality (psychosis). These in turn lead to expressions of anger, violence, agitation and fear, as well as compulsive, manipulative and anti-social behaviour, which are very disabling handicaps.

Those with mental handicaps possess the pains of the heart as well as the gifts of the heart. They present a challenge as well as a gift to those of us who live at the level of the intellect and can so easily conceal our real needs from others and even from ourselves. Their gift is to reveal the true humanity that we share: the same deep need to be loved and to love, to belong and to be valued for who we are, to choose, to have the opportunity to develop our full potential, and to reach out and touch the spiritual.

It can be threatening to recognize those needs we take trouble to conceal, clearly manifested by people with whom we might prefer not to identify, "people we are here to help." The Jesuit, John Powell, expressed the fear this engenders:[29] "I am afraid to tell you who I am, because, if I tell you who I am, you may not like who I am, and it's all that I have."

The vocation and vulnerability of assistants

It is extremely stressful to live or work for long hours alongside people whose profound suffering is expressed in demanding and disturbing ways. Assistants have often experienced personal loss and deprivation, albeit usually in less dramatic ways: their wounds, whatever their nature, and however deeply buried in the unconscious, resonate with those of people who are mentally handicapped. This can result in an awareness of painful and angry feelings in the assistant, the cause of which is more complex and deep-seated than mere annoyance or impatience.

As children, we all develop defence mechanisms in order to survive traumatic events, perhaps by suppressing the memory of their existence, and these mechanisms are reactivated when we are confronted with the demanding needs of others, which in some way relate to those childhood experiences of suffering.

An assistant needs to be clear about personal identity in order to live and work for any length of time with men and women with mental handicaps whose experience of suffering lies close to the surface, and may be regularly manifested in disturbing and demanding behaviour. He or she needs to have a human maturity with a healthy understanding of their own gifts, skills and limitations. Such an understanding enables the "care-giver" to have a proper appreciation of themselves as a person with legitimate needs who requires space and time in which to meet those needs. One who has achieved this level of maturity can recognize that

---

29   John Powell, *Why Am I Afraid To Tell You Who I Am?* (Collins, Fount, 1978), p. 7.

other assistants and mentally handicapped people also have legitimate needs and must be given the time and space in which to meet them.

As assistants, we are frequently attracted to l'Arche by the warm welcome we find and, at least in the early days, we are prepared to invest the whole of ourselves in generous and compassionate caring. It takes time and considerable humility to accept the need for personal development and to begin to see how our own needs can result in unhealthy dynamics: "compulsive caring," the need to be needed, and subtle ways of controlling and manipulating others. These are the hazards of any caring situation and not something particular to l'Arche. However, anyone living in a caring situation which is sometimes more akin to "24 hours a day" than the usual nine-to-five working day is particularly vulnerable in this respect, because such a way of life can frequently involve the entire affective lives of those concerned, the heart becoming much more involved than the intellect which might otherwise exercise a necessarily restraining role.

We have to be ready to accept moments when we feel completely powerless alongside the suffering of another, and this requires proper support and understanding so that the experience may be integrated into our own personal development and, for Christians, into our understanding of the gospel. In many ways l'Arche seeks to re-empower powerless people, and the redistribution of power, like the redistribution of wealth, requires those who have the most to part with some of it. The deep significance of such redistribution needs to be developed for those who experience it: mentally handicapped people who are being "empowered" and assistants and others who are thus required to "lose" or share their power.

Psychotherapy and many forms of counselling have enabled us to recognize that greater awareness of our unconscious selves is a gift of God to be wisely used. It is part of becoming more fully human, as is that life at the level of the heart to which people with mental handicaps invite us.

Christian community, like any community based on belief in a supreme being who is known as creator and sustainer, is a place in which we can learn to love – a place in which our love can begin to be refined, purified and truly aligned with the love of God.

To love is to accept "the other" as he or she is – different from myself. Communities of l'Arche are privileged places in which to learn to love, because life alongside those who live at the level of the heart reveals our deepest needs and our vulnerability, while inviting us to consider what it is to be fully human. Within l'Arche we have the possibility of real interdependence; which has been described as a mutuality of vocation, the mutual enabling of the assistant and the person with a mental handicap.

God has "hidden things from the wise and understanding and revealed them to mere children" (Luke 10:21) and "God chose what is weak in the world to shame the strong" (1 Corinthians 1:27). We believe in the capacity of the weak and of mere children to touch and change the hearts of people and thus to foster unity, but in our communities we know something of the personal cost involved in releasing the gifts of the poor to help heal the wounds of the churches and of humanity. It is this mutuality of vocation which is part of the contribution of l'Arche to ecumenism.

Our ecumenical vocation – a way of unity open to all

There are barriers to unity between the Christian churches and between different Faiths caused by cultural differences and difficulties in human relationships which are much more substantial than differences of teaching or belief.

In a talk given to leaders of l'Arche communities in North America in 1988, Tom Ryan said:

> The unity of the Church has to do profoundly with the quality of our lives together as Christians. Hence that unity must involve the breaking down of barriers erected by sexism, by classism, by racism and by disrespect for life, whether of the handicapped, the unborn or the aged: realities which are in the church as well as in the world.
>
> If Christian communities are to serve as parables of unity for the human family, they must evolve models of leadership and styles of life together in which sharing power with the powerless becomes a reality, and in which servanthood and the symbol of the wounded healer are dominant.

We have all wounded each other through prejudice and judgement, through lack of respect and lack of love. We all need the same humility and the ability to forgive, whether we are members of l'Arche communities or church leaders responsible for ecumenical dialogue.

In his book *Crossing the Threshold to Hope,* Pope John Paul II writes in response to the question "Why did the Holy Spirit permit all these divisions [between Christians]?":[30]

> There are two possible answers to this question. The more negative one would see in these divisions the bitter fruit of sins committed by Christians. The more positive answer is inspired by trust in the One who is capable of bringing forth good even from evil, from human weakness. Could it not be that these divisions have also been a path continually leading the Church to discover the untold wealth contained in Christ's Gospel and in the redemption accomplished by Christ? Perhaps all this wealth would not have come to light otherwise. . . .

and

> It is necessary for humanity to achieve unity through plurality, to learn to come together in the one Church, even while presenting a plurality of ways of thinking and acting, of cultures and civilizations.

In l'Arche we have learned that a desire to respect each person in our communities includes not only respect for their religious beliefs, but also for the churches and other religious bodies to which they belong. However complex the issues raised by the diversity of our belonging, we are conscious that we are enriched by the gifts which come from our different religious traditions; these are an integral part of the spirit in which we seek to live. This sense of gift has been developed in *Ecumenism in l'Arche* (1), but could be summarized as follows: the centrality of eucharistic celebrations in the Roman Catholic Church not only

---

[30]   London: Jonathan Cape, 1994, p. 153.

nourishes our Roman Catholic communities, but in interdenominational communities has led to a deepening search for the full meaning of the sacrament and its relationship to the washing of the feet on the night before Christ's passion.

Anglicanism has provided a particularly relevant model of inclusiveness and of holding differences in creative tension. God's truth is always greater than our understanding of it.

Churches of the Reformation emphasize that it is the *people* who constitute the church and l'Arche is deeply concerned to build community with a similar emphasis. Many marks of the Reformed churches find resonance in l'Arche. We recognize the importance of their example of fellowship in the fact that l'Arche stresses the significance of such community-building activities as shared prayer, visits, meetings and celebrations.

In our contacts with members of Orthodox Churches we are given a particular sense of the sacred in worship.

In our communities in India both Christians and Hindus can articulate their respect for the fact that God is present in all creation, which leads towards principles of non-violence and universal brotherhood. This is a particular gift of Hinduism.

But the barriers of division are very powerful and are often maintained by deep-seated fears, anguish and anger; they are not easily overcome, but demand a real and painful relinquishing of self-interest, a purifying of motives. Such a *metanoia* or conversion can only happen through self-giving: for Christians, to the person of Jesus; for members of other Faiths, to the focus of unity and love which is their source of life.

If friendship and trust are so important, then relationships and the challenge of learning to love are particularly relevant. Perhaps this is more especially so in the Western churches where, historically (except within limited circles), the accent has almost always been on moral and dogmatic teaching, rather than on the experience of a relationship with God. Today there is an increasing hunger for such a relationship among Christians and those of other Faiths and it is frequently manifested in a desire to discover new ways of prayer. Christians of all denominations are participating together in this search for a living spirituality which underlines the importance of *relationship*.

In l'Arche our experience tells us that those who live at the level of the heart challenge and open us to what it means to be fully human, and part of this is the revelation of our need for relationship with God. People with handicaps reveal the true nature of the beatitudes in Christ's sermon on the mount (Luke 6:20-23):

"Blessed are you poor [always dependent on others, devoid of intellectual defences and escapes], for yours is the kingdom of God";

"Blessed are you that hunger now [for unconditional love, undivided attention, recognition, affirmation], for you shall be satisfied";

"Blessed are you that weep now [because you feel unwanted, different, useless and lost], for you shall laugh";

"Blessed are you when men hate you, and they exclude you and revile you [for that has often been your experience]."[31]

Our common humanity

Acknowledging our vulnerability can bring us closer to one another in our personal brokenness, in the brokenness of the wider body of the Church and in the brokenness of humanity.

The second-century bishop, Saint Irenaeus, wrote: "The glory of God is the human being fully alive."[32] We live in an age in which we are increasingly losing sight of what it really means to be human. The forces which foster this negative development are very powerful, yet at the same time there are voices which call us to hope in the future of humanity, as there are signs that some among us are struggling to become fully human, fully alive, and more deeply united with fellow human beings. People with mental handicaps are sometimes ahead of the rest of us in this.

The Jesuit palæontologist and anthropologist, Teilhard de Chardin, believed that men and women were still on an evolutionary path of transformation, the slow transformation into the fullness of their humanity and their capacity to love as God loves

---

[31]   See the Dedication, p. v.
[32]   *Adversus Haereses*, IV, xx, 6.

us: "The day will come when, after harnessing space, the winds, the tides and gravitation, We shall harness for God the energies of love. And on that day, for the second time in the history of the world, we shall have discovered fire."[33]

The last words of Jesus to his disciples before entering into his passion were in the form of a prayer to his Father: ". . . that they may all be one.... that they may be one as we are one.... that the love with which thou has loved me may be in them, and I in them" (John 17:21-26). This surely is a prayer for "unity according to the model of the Holy Trinity, in profound respect for one another, seeking neither to absorb nor isolate the different, but holding each one in the true balance and poise of love."[34] The call of Jesus for unity is a call to believe that the Spirit is working within others who are different, within churches in their diversity, so that each can learn from the other the ways of the Spirit.

The energy of love has a great deal to do with communion, that very deep relationship for which the human heart longs. In l'Arche we believe that people with mental handicaps and their assistants have a part to play in transforming the world by love – no matter how tiny their contribution may appear. The journey is long, but the fact that we are trying to build community with those who so greatly need harmony and unity within relationships can help us all.

People who live at the level of the heart can be catalysts of unity, though we know that they can also destroy it. How can we enable men and women with mental handicaps to be creators rather than destroyers? The poet T. S. Eliot wrote: "Humankind cannot bear very much reality" ("Burnt Norton," *Four Quartets*). Sometimes the needy cry of another is too painful to bear, so we draw back and are unable to help the other to grow through a particular experience. Very practical ways forward can be of assistance here:

- The willingness to belong to a supportive team or a community that is aware of the urgent need for unity experienced by

---

[33] "The Evolution of Chastity" (1934), in *Towards the Future* (New York: Harcourt Brace Jovanovich, 1975), quoted in Blanche Gallagher, ed., *Meditations with Teil- hard de Chardin* (Sante Fe, New Mexico: Bear & Co., 1988), p. 133.

[34] *Ecumenism in l'Arche* (2), p. 19.

those they care for and will therefore take steps to ensure that the team or community are united among themselves.

- The recognition of the needy child within ourselves and the willingness to learn to share our vulnerability while being honest and realistic about our own needs and allowing ourselves and others to meet them.
- The willingness to recognize the real significance of caring and relating to the needy person when we may be tempted to dismiss what we are trying to do as "a waste of time." In l'Arche we speak of "hearing the call of God in the poor."
- The willingness to spend time with men and women with mental handicaps or others who live at the level of the heart in order to discover how to relate non-verbally: the appropriate use of touch and how to convey love and acceptance by our presence and our expression. This involves us in learning to bow down before the mystery of another human being and thus before the mystery of God.

With the necessary support and insight, with an understanding of God's place in our experience, we can listen attentively to the cry of the other person, respond to it creatively, and even be renewed by it. This willingness to respond in a way that invites harmony and unity around the needy person is illustrated by two stories, one from England and the other from Africa. Tony, the local Methodist minister, and his wife Christine, were having supper in a community household. Afterwards, while people were washing up, Laurence, who has a severe mental handicap and does not speak, became bored and fractious. He took a guitar and began strumming in a noisy, tuneless way. After a moment Christine began to pick out a tune on another guitar. Through their combined offering there was music and when they finished, there was a round of applause. A smile spread from one side of Laurence's face to the other. Tony said that he saw, for the first time, what it meant to "grin from ear to ear." They began playing again and others joined in with percussion instruments and humming; this went on for quite a long time.

Christine responded to Laurence's desire to "make music" by quietly joining in more tunefully. This drew on the good will of others in the room. Laurence was affirmed and had achieved his aim not only to "make music," but to draw people into unity around him. One can imagine a very different ending to the evening if the initial response by Christine or anyone else had been negative.

The second story comes from Nongr Maasem, the l'Arche community in West Africa in Ouagadougou, where we welcome children with mental handicaps. Bertrand describes the Friday evening eucharist after a long and tiring week: "We are hot and many of us assistants arrive late. The children are tired and dirty, but *they* arrive on time because they always love the celebration of the eucharist. Denis generally falls asleep, but wakes up towards the end. We sing the 'L'Arche in Africa' song without much enthusiasm, and at the back of the chapel Denis gets to his feet. His timing is perfect. He comes to stand before the altar and begins to dance. The assistants at first find it rather tiresome to be 'woken up,' but then we look at each other, smile, laugh, clap our hands and play the tom-toms with vigour and conviction. Denis has a huge smile and is very happy indeed. In his simplicity and his love of celebration he knows how to give thanks and how to communicate his love for us and for God. Humanity means sharing your joy with all those around you. Every Friday Denis reminds us, in the presence of Jesus, of what it means to be truly human."

The Jesuit, Patrick Purnell, wrote of the cry of God as a new-born infant:

The Christ-child tumbled
into the world
head-first,
caught by a nimble mid-wife,
felicitously,
who thumped him,
promptly,
to gulp the air
and cry;
this was the first known sound
of God
in the world.

Those who live at the level of their hearts continue to echo "the first known sound of God in the world." The sound may be distorted, it may disturb us, but let us not walk away from it, for it is the cry of our own hearts.

7

One bread

The cup of blessing which we bless, is it not a participation in the blood of Christ? The bread which we break, is it not a participation in the body of Christ? Because there is one bread, we who are many are one body, for we all partake of the one bread. (1 Corinthians 10:16-17)

The context in which Paul was writing to the men and women of Corinth suggests a pluralistic society with complex laws and demands, men and women who were unclear about where they belonged and were struggling with conflicting demands and needs.

During the Anglican eucharist the celebrant says: "We break this bread to share in the body of Christ," and I respond, "Though we are many, we are one body, because we all share in one bread."[35] In saying these words I am fully aware that we live in a very similar situation to that of the Corinthians two thousand years ago. We too live in a pluralistic society, unclear about where we belong, and struggling with complex laws and conflicting demands and needs. Obviously our communities do not escape these constraints, but feel them deeply. Although I say "we all share in one bread," I must then ask to be blessed rather than sharing in that one bread. And I ask myself, Why do I go on saying these words? What is this bread which I share, yet do not share?

---

[35]   Rite A, *The Alternative Service Book*, Church of England, 1980.

At the Anglican eucharist the words of the Our Father, "Give us this day our daily bread," come immediately before the words of St. Paul, and this has begun to give meaning to the contradiction I have been experiencing. In the King James version of the Bible I find Paul's words rendered: "For we being many, are *one bread, and one body:* for we are all partakers of that one bread." That small difference in translation gives a different picture: "*We* are one bread." The bread we share in our communities is daily life both as an extension of the eucharist and as a path leading to the celebration of the eucharist. The words of Stephen Verney underlined the fact that the bread we share is our common humanity. "You are *eucharistic* communities: take the bread, receive the bread which each of you is for the other, give thanks and bless – experiencing the brokenness within you – give this bread that you are to one another."

When Nick blessed the bread and water (p. 58) and shared it at supper with his companions in daily life, he did so because of his sense of something lacking among us as a community: a separation which was at its clearest and most painful at the time of the community eucharists and when we went our separate ways to our different churches on Sunday morning. Nick acted as he did in the context of daily life and his gesture enabled us all – Nick included – to deepen our understanding of the relationship between the eucharist and daily life: the daily bread which we seek to give and share in remembrance of Jesus.

After each community eucharist we distribute loaves of bread to each community household as a reminder to each one of the eucharistic link between daily life and daily bread. In each community household the loaf is destined to be shared at an ordinary meal as part of daily life.

We are also called to share *ourselves* with those who are afflicted: those who are oppressed, poor, in prison, hungry, thirsty, naked, or in any other sort of need. "First share the bread of affliction and only then the bread of the eucharist." For most people, and certainly for our communities, the sharing of the "bread" that is ourselves is far from dramatic. People are thirsty for attention, hungry because they are lonely and sad, they are "prisoners" because they are old, ill or disabled and cannot get out, or imprisoned by the lack of any sense of their own value, "naked" and therefore vulnerable because they feel blamed for or guilty of "misdeeds" which they may not in fact have committed.

Here surely is to be found "the bread of affliction" of which Donald Nicholl writes. Would it be surprising to find among the poor and oppressed the point of convergence for those seeking unity? Our priority has always been the welcome of people whose affliction and pain lies in the fact that they do not fit into our different societies. These people are at the heart of our communities, regardless of the probable diversity of religious affiliation, because we believe that their place there takes precedence over unity in Faith or unity at the eucharist.

In our communities the sharing of ourselves as "bread" for one another is a process in which each one enables that other to follow the call of God, to follow his or her personal vocation. To give just one example of such mutual enabling: Antoine Koua-goué of the l'Arche community in West Africa at Bouaké on Ivory Coast describes his friendship with Koffi Bragon:

> My friend Koffi was born, like me, in 1962. His early life in his family was traumatic because of his mental handicap and epilepsy. Our combined story began in 1984 when the leader of our community asked me to teach Koffi to read and write. When I agreed I had no idea what I was committing myself to.
>
> During our meetings I discovered his great need to be loved and to find unity and harmony around him. I felt challenged to undertake a truthful and faithful relationship with him. Koffi was looking for a friend who would listen to him and would accept to live with him.
>
> Koffi had often expressed a wish to deepen his faith. We helped to prepare him for baptism in 1992. His life seemed transformed. He always joins in times of prayer in the community. He helps me to hear the call of God and to pray, so as to live my faith to the full.
>
> In 1994 Koffi participated in the l'Arche in Africa time of Renewal for people with handicaps, because, he said, "I want to live in greater harmony in the community." I shared his joy and his sadness as together we first visited his family and then re-told his story at the Renewal. He was able to say

Koffi Bragon and Antoine Kouagoué at l'Arche Bouaké

how hard it is to be different, to have to give up ideas of marriage and having a family. He accepts himself today as he is. This was a time of healing for him because he realized that if he is handicapped it is not his fault. I give thanks for being witness to his journey.

In accepting necessary changes within his own family and in our community, Koffi is now a man of wisdom, a source of peace and unity. His very presence calls us to be artisans of love that is true and faithful.

Many in our world are struggling towards racial, sexual, religious, social or political reconciliation and unity. At the same time there is a deeply rooted resistance to the implications of such a struggle: one cannot get away from the fact that if wealth, power, and status are to be shared, then those who possess these benefits must part with something. There are mixed motives in each one of us – rich and poor – in the attempt to welcome difference and diversity; we cannot escape the concrete difficulties this involves and the "blockages" we find within ourselves, all of which are part of the messiness and fragility of being human.

Our communities are, at least to some extent, microcosms of the world around. However, they are distinguished from it by the centrality of people who live at the level of the heart and reveal to themselves and to others the fundamental human need to be loved and to love, to be valued and to belong.

> L'Arche communities are communities of faith, rooted in prayer and trust in God. They seek to be guided by God and by their weakest members, through whom God's presence is revealed. Each community member is encouraged to discover and deepen his or her spiritual life and live it according to his or her particular faith and tradition. Those who have no religious affiliation are welcomed and respected in their freedom of conscience. (Charter of l'Arche III.1.1)

Within our communities, the search for reconciliation and unity among ourselves has always transcended the question of "unity among Christians of different traditions" or "unity between Christians and members of other Faiths," because we seek unity with everyone of goodwill. In the early days we asked assistants "to be willing to respect and learn to love people with mental handicaps." Today I believe we might express this requirement in terms of the need "to be willing to learn how to become more fully human through a shared life with people who live at the level of their hearts."

The nature of our communities and our determination to be an international "family" incorporating a disconcerting diversity of individuals convinces me that the only thing uniting us is our common humanity. The strengths and weaknesses of such a "broad-brush" position have significant implications for all those living in our communities. Most significantly there must be a deep unity among the teams of assistants in households, work-shops and in leadership roles, whatever their differences in terms of race, religion and moral stance. The inner disturbance and bro-kenness in the people with mental handicaps results from an experience of life which has often been extremely painful. This leaves them with a powerful and urgent need to discover that the world, frequently represented by the assistants around them, is in fact a safe and harmonious place, contrary to the messages received through previous experience.

Assistants are therefore required to give priority to the crea-tion of unity within themselves and with others, with all that this implies in terms of personal development towards maturity and gift of self. Adequate support and formation are required in order that assistants may work towards and finally achieve these goals while living creatively within the demands and stresses of daily life.

The search for unity with everyone of goodwill involves us in trying to live with difference in a way that is creative and unthreatening to ourselves or others. We have to contend with differing moral values and can take nothing for granted in terms of the convictions and attitudes of those who come to the com-munities, as assistants, visitors, or individuals with mental hand-icaps.

Ethical and moral issues involving fundamental values may need to be defined and resolved by people who hold very dif-ferent views. Within l'Arche experience has shown that, as such a dialogue proceeds, respect and concern for the needs of community members with mental handicaps gradually becomes a guiding factor. This recognition of the needs of very vulnerable people at the heart of the community takes precedence over other considerations and enables people of goodwill, who nevertheless hold differing views, to reach a consensus. Thus men and women with mental handicaps can be the means of forging a unity which would not otherwise be considered, let alone achieved.

I believe that by putting the needs of those who live at the level of the heart *at the centre*, we may finally reach a decision which, at the time, is not necessarily experienced as being to the greater benefit of the powerful and persuasive, but can be seen to be more *human*. Such a decision frequently relates to values pertaining to individual and communal behaviour which have been generally subscribed to by members of the main World Faiths until the second half of the twentieth century. Throughout the world today there is deep concern about "the values of our society" – how these can be re-established, respected and conveyed. I believe that in listening to the voices of those who live at the level of the heart there can be the beginning of a new wisdom: a re-statement of fundamental human values.

It has been said that civilisations can be judged by the way in which they treat their weakest members. I would go further and say that the weakest members can enable a civilisation to become more fully human by the recognition that the needs and aspirations of the weakest members are in fact the needs and aspirations of all. It is then a question of how to meet these needs and counter the obstacles we meet in the process.

Values which derive from an over-dependence upon market forces, or from isolating independence may appear inhuman, but there are signs of hope when it comes to values relating to human rights and freedoms and care in the community, even if the language frequently used, such as "consumer choice" or "client-led appraisal," smacks of the market place rather than pastoral concern. I believe that these human values can be fostered by communities such as l'Arche and others who live alongside, work with and care for vulnerable people.

It will, however, be a slow process since fundamental change is required in terms of the surrendering of attitudes of domination and power in order that we may listen to the voices of the powerless. This is not a simple matter, as I pointed out in Chapter 6, since such voices may be faint, angry, inarticulate, confused, manipulated or manipulating... and it may take considerable time to understand the deepest, and therefore most fully human, desires of the weakest members of society.

In the end I believe that among the most important human values to be rediscovered in this way are freedom, responsibility, fidelity, wholeness, maturity and an interdependence which implies unity. Could it be that in struggling to be more fully human, we are beginning to listen more intently to the words of St. Paul?: "Those whom the world thinks common and contemptible are the ones that God has chosen – those who are nothing at all to show up those who are everything" (1 Corinthians 1:28; Jerusalem Bible).

Modern technology daily reveals to us the interdependence within the animal and plant worlds, and between those worlds and human beings. As human beings we discover how little we have cared for the earth. Some interpretations of modern physics speak of sub-atomic particles not as isolated grains of matter, but as dynamic interrelations and interactions between the parts, their interrelationship being more fundamental than the parts themselves. The implication is that interrelationship and interdependence exist at the level of the tiniest "building blocks" of creation. Yet when it comes to humanity, at least in the West, we find today an increasing tendency to glorify the individual and laud *independence* at the expense of interdependence.

The presence of the weak at the heart of our communities therefore enables us to become more fully human by restoring the neglected balance between heart and intellect, heart and head. There is an increasing danger that without men and women who operate primarily at the level of the heart, we will lose sight of the fact that the most profound human needs stem from the heart, and that the greatest human fulfilment lies in the domain of the heart.

After a visit to Faith and Light communities in Rwanda at the end of 1995, Jean Vanier wrote:

During the celebration of the eucharist for about twenty mothers with their handicapped children and friends, all quite poor, many of them widows whose husbands had been killed during the massacres, the women came up to the altar at the offertory and offered their children to God. I almost cried. Several women spoke of all they had discovered about their own child through Faith and Light. They told me about a family with a handicapped son. When the militia came to take the family away, the son went out to meet them with outstretched arms. The militia went away.

Listen, my beloved brethren, has not God chosen those who are poor in the world to be rich in faith and heirs to the kingdom which he has promised to those who love him?" (James 2:5)

Appendix

Further examples
of domestic liturgies [36]

Lent and Easter

Each Friday in Lent our community gathers at a different home to have a simple meal of soup and cheese. Each person is encouraged to bring a gift of money which this year was given to care for orphans of the Iraqi war. Gifts of food are brought by each home and given to a local group caring for the homeless.

After supper some members of the community remain for the Taizé Vigil of the Cross, modelled after the practice of the ecumenical community at Taizé in France. People kneel or sit around the cross laid on the floor. In turn they place their foreheads on the cross, giving to Jesus all the sufferings of the world which they carry in their minds and hearts.

L'Arche Erie, Pennsylvania

On Easter morning an hour and a half before sunrise all community members and friends get dressed and drive to the top of Mount Royal, the mountain at the heart of Montreal. We gather at the foot of the illuminated cross and together wait for sunrise, singing and listening to music. After the joyful songs at sunrise, we gather at a makeshift table on which there is wine and bread made by community members. We share some scripture read-

---

[36] These are taken from "Celebrate Our Unity." Further information about this can be obtained from Daybreak Publications, 11339 Yonge St., Richmond Hill, Ontario, Canada L4S 1L1.

ings in English and French then we pray for a short while, ending with "Hail to the Risen Lord." We then break the bread and drink the wine.

Then we go for Easter breakfast together. Before we eat each person receives an Easter egg which contains a message drawn from the Bible; we all hold up our eggs and say: "Jesus is risen," then break the eggs, read our message, and help those around to read their messages. We bless the meal, eat our breakfast and then we go to our respective parishes to continue to celebrate Easter.

L'Arche Montreal, Canada

Regular events

Bread sharing has been a tradition in our Shalom community for the past twelve years. To start with, enough bread is baked for each household and family in the community by one household or family each week. While the bread is being made, the "bakers" pray for each member of the community and the needs of the community as a whole.

The bread is brought to our office on Mondays and assistants pray as they distribute bread to a person from each home. The same evening there is a simple meal in each house in solidarity with those in the world who have little to eat. The community bread is broken and shared. After grace we say together the scripture passage: "Though we are many we are one body, for we all partake of the one loaf." The bread is passed, usually in silence, each one breaking a piece and handing it to the next.

L'Arche Edmonton, Alberta, Canada

On Fridays after prayer, we have our house meeting. After the house meeting, all of us make a huddle – arms around each other – the prayer table being in the middle. We sing: "Heal us, Jesus, thank you, Jesus." We have a moment of silence. Then we give the kiss of peace to each other. This is symbolic of a New Beginning and of asking Jesus to heal each of us of the hurts and pain we might have caused each other during the week.

Irenicon Community, Bradford, Massachusetts

Birthdays

Birthdays:... after the meal and while we eat the cake, the birthday person tells the story of how he or she came to l'Arche. Each person is then encouraged to say how the birthday person has been a gift to them over the past year. This exchange has a really sacred element to it. As we hear how one life has touched the life of another, we experience the presence of God. The "party" becomes a celebration of thanksgiving for the birth of our special friend who is then asked to say how they have been a gift to themselves. We end with prayer.

L'Arche Calgary, Alberta, Canada

Special Events

Gandhi Jayanti (Gandhi's birthday), October 2nd. Every year we honour Mahatma Gandhi and are inspired by his life. We set up prayer with his picture at the centre, sing Indian *bhajans*, burn incense, have oil lamps and any symbols from India we can find. Someone shares about Gandhi, his life and his message. We pray for the communities in India.[37]

L'Arche Cape Breton, Whycocomagh, Nova Scotia, Canada

---

[37] Some community members had spent several years in the Indian communities.

Bibliography

* *Blessing at the Time of Communion*, L'Arche U.K. Pastoral Ecumenical Committee, 1995.

Celebrate Our Unity, L'Arche North America Commission on Ecumenism, 1992.

Celibacy and the Single Life in l'Arche, Donald Allchin (A. M. Allchin), L'Arche Europe Commission on Ecumenism, 1993.

* *An Ecumenical Journey – l'Arche in the U.K.*, Thérèse Vanier, 1989.

* *Ecumenism in l'Arche* (1), International Council of l'Arche, 1995.

* *Ecumenism in l'Arche* (2), International Council of l'Arche, 1995.

Eucharistic Hospitality, L'Arche Europe-Africa-Middle East Commission on Ecumenism, 1990.

Guidelines for Working with Local Parishes, Maggie Smith, L'Arche Europe Commission on Ecumenism, 1991.

Guidelines on Organising Retreats, L'Arche Europe Commission on Ecumenism, 1992.

Healing a Wound, l'Arche U.K. Pastoral Ecumenical Committee, 1992 (available in *Ecumenism in l'Arche* [2]).

L'Arche – A Way of Unity Open to All People, L'Arche Europe-Africa-Middle East Commission on Ecumenism, 1990 (available in *Ecumenism in l'Arche* [2]).

Nick: Man of the Heart, Thérèse Vanier, Gill & Macmillan, 1993.

Partners in Life, The Handicapped and the Church, ed. Geiko Muller-Fahrenholz, Faith and Order Paper No. 89, World Council of Churches, Geneva, 1979.

Reflections on Celibacy and Chastity, Sister Hélène, L'Arche Europe Commission on Ecumenism, 1993.

The Reservation of the Blessed Sacrament, Donald Allchin (A. M. Allchin), L'Arche Europe Commission on Ecumenism, 1993.

The Testing of Hearts: A Pilgrim's Journal, Donald Nicholl, Lamp Press, 1989 (obtainable from: Mrs. Nicholl, Rostherne, Common Lane, Betley, Crewe, Cheshire, CW3 9AL, England).

The Unity of the Church and the Handicapped in Society, Study Encounter 17, Vol. VII, No. 4, Faith and Order Commission, World Council of Churches, 1971.

* Available from L'Arche U.K. Secretariat, 10 Briggate, Silsden, Keighley, West Yorkshire, BD20 9JT, England.

MARQUIS

PRINTED BY
IMPRIMERIE D'ÉDITION MARQUIS
IN FEBRUARY 1997
MONTMAGNY (QUÉBEC)